1 MONTH OF
FREE
READING

at

www.ForgottenBooks.com

By purchasing this book you are eligible for one month membership to ForgottenBooks.com, giving you unlimited access to our entire collection of over 1,000,000 titles via our web site and mobile apps.

To claim your free month visit:

www.forgottenbooks.com/free898131

ISBN 978-0-265-84507-3
PIBN 10898131

rir	d	Inuencyon of the crosse	iij
biij	e	Festum corone spine domini	iiij
	f	saynt Godarde	b
rbi	g	saynt Johan ante portam latinam	bi
b		saynt Johan of Beuarlay	bij
	b	apperynge of saynt Myghell.	biij
riij	c	Transl.of saynt Nycholas	ir
ij	d	saynt Gordine and Epimach	r
	e	saynt Anthony martyr	ri
r	f	Nerei/achilei/and pancratij	rij
	g	Seruatius confessour	riij
rbiij		The Sonne in Gemini	riiij
bij	b	saynt Ilpdore martyr	rb
	c	saynt Brandyne byschop	rbi
rb	d	Transl.of saynt Bernarde	rbij
iiij	e	saynt Dioscor martyr	rbiij
	f	saynt Dunstani byschop and côfessour	rir
rij	g	saynt Bernardine.	rr
i		Helyne quene	rri
	b	Julyane birgyn	rrij
ir	c	saynt Desyderij martyr	rriij
	d	transl.of saynt Franceys	rriiij
rbij	e	saynt Aldelme byschoppe	rrb
bi	f	saynt austayne	rrbi
	g	saynt Bede preest	rrbij
riiij		saynt Germayne byschoppe	rrbiij
iij	b	saynt corone martyr	rrir
	c	saynt felyr byschop of Rome	rrr
ri	d	Petronille birgyn.	rrri

IVNIVS;

In June all thyng falleth to rypenesse,
And so dooth man at .xxxvi. yere olde,
And studyeth for to acquyre rychesse.
And taketh a wyfe to kepe his housholde.

IN June. The nyght is .v. houres. And
the day is .xvi. houres.

   e Necomede martyr

xix f Marcellyne and Peter

i
ij

biij	g	ſaynt Eraſmus	iij
rbi		ſaynt petroce	iiij
b	b	Bonyface and his felowes	b
	c	Mellone archbyſſhoppe	bi
riij	d	Tranſlacyon of ſ. wlſtane	bij
ij	e	Mederde and gilderde	biij
	f	Tranſlacyon of ſ. Edmunde	ir
r	g	puon confeſſour	r
		Barnabe apoſtle	ri
rbiij	b	Baſylyde / neryne / ⁊ nabo.	rij
bij	c	Anthony.	riij
	d	Baſily byſſhoppe	riiij
rb	e	Wyte / Modeſte ⁊ creſcenty	rb
iiij	f	Tranſlacyon of ſaynt rycharde	rbi
	g	Saynt botulphe	rbij
rij		Marcelly and marcylian	rbiij
i	b	Geruaſy and Prothaſy	rir
	c	Tranſlacyon of ſ. Edwarde	rr
ir	d	walburge birgyn	rri
	e	ſaynt Albane martyr	rrij
rbij	f	Saynt Audrye Wygyll	rriij
bi	g		rriiij
		Tranſlacyon of elegy byſ.	rrb
riiij	b	Johñ and Paule	rrbi
iij	c	Saynt creſcent	rrbij
	d	Leo byſſhop of Rome	rrbiij
ri	e		rrir
	f	Commemoracyon of Paule	rrr

At .xl. yere of aege oz elles neuer
Is ony man ende wed with wyſdome.
Foz than fozthon his myght fayleth euer.
As in July dooth euery bloſſome.

In July.The nyght is .biij. houres / and
the day is .rbj. houres.
rir g Octa. Iohñ baptyſt
biij A Viſytacyon of our Lady

i

ij

	b	Tranſlacyon of Thomas apoſtle⳿	iij
ꞃbj	c	Tranſlacyon of ſaynt martin⳿	iiij
b	d	Zoe virgyn and martyꝛ	v
	e	Octa⳿apoſt⳿peter and paule⳿	vj
ꞃiij	f	Tranſlacyon of Thomas martyꝛ	vij
ij	g	Depoſicyon of ſaynt grymbalde	viij
	A	Cirylly byſſhoppe	iꞃ
ꞃ	b	Seuen bꞃether martyꝛs	ꞃ
	c	Tranſlacyon of ſaynt benet	ꞃj
ꞃviij	d	Naboꝛ and felyꞃ	ꞃij
vij	e	Pꞃiuate martyꝛ	ꞃiij
	f	The Dinte in Lee	ꞃiiij
ꞃv	g	Tranſlacyon of ſaynt ſwythune	ꞃv
iiij	A	Saynt oſmunde	ꞃvj
	b	Kenelme kynge	ꞃvij
ꞃij	c	Arnulphe byſſhop⳿	ꞃviij
i	d	Ruſyne and Juſtyne	ꞃiꞃ
	e	Saynt margaret virgyn⳿	ꞃꞃ
iꞃ	f	Pꞃaxede virgyn⳿	ꞃꞃj
	g	Mary magdalene	ꞃꞃij
ꞃvij	A	Appolynarius byſſhoppe⳿	ꞃꞃiij
vj	b	Chꞃyſtyne virgyn⳿ Vigyll⳿	ꞃꞃiiij
	c	James apoſtle ſ⳿Chꞃyſtofer⳿	ꞃꞃv
ꞃiiij	d	Anne mother of our Lady	ꞃꞃvj
iij	e	The ſeuen ſlepers	ꞃꞃvij
	f	Sampſon byſſhoppe	ꞃꞃviij
ꞃj	g	Felyꞃ and his felowes	ꞃꞃiꞃ
ꞃiꞃ	A	Abdon and ſennes	ꞃꞃꞃ
	b	Germayne byſſhoppe⳿	ꞃꞃꞃj

AVGVSTVS

The goodes of the erthe is gadied euer moie.
In august/so at.xl viij.yere.
Man ought to gather some goodes in stoie.
To susteyne aege that than diaweth nere.

BII august. The nyght is.ⁱ.houres/and
the daye is.xiiij.houres.

viij   c Lammas daye   i

xvi   d Saynt Stephan byſhop of Rome   ij

Auguſt.

b	e	Inuencyon of ſaynt Stephan	iij
	f	ſaynt Juſtyne pzeeſt	iiij
riij	g	Feſtum niuis	v
ij		¶ Tranſfy.of our lozde	vj
	b	The feaſt of Jeſu	vij
r	c	ſaynt Ciryake and his felowes	viij
	d	ſaynt Romayne martyz	ir
rviij	e	ſaynt Laurence martyz	r
vij	f	ſaynt tyburcyus martyz	ri
	g	ſaynt Clare virgyn	rij
rb		¶ ſaynt ypolyte and his felowes	riij
iiij	b	Euſebius Uigyll.	riiij
	c	The aſſumpcyon of our lady	rb
rij	d	ſaynt Rocke. ¶ The Stone Uigy	rbj
i	e	octaues of ſaynt Laurence	rbij
	f	ſaynt Agapite martyz	rbiij
ir	g	ſaynt Magnus martyz	rir
		¶ ſaynt Lewys martyz	rr
rvj	b	ſaynt bernarde abbot	rri
vj	c	octa.aſſumpcyon	rrij
	d	Timothei Uigyll	rriij
riiij	e	Bartholmewe apoſtle	rriiij
iij	f	ſaynt Lewys kynge	rrb
	g	ſaynt Seueryne	rrbj
ri		¶ ſaynt Ruſe martyz	rrbij
rir	b	Caput Auſtayne	rrbiij
	c	Decollacyon of ſaynt Johan	rrir
viij	d	ſaynt felyr and adaucte	rrr
	e	ſaynt Cuthburge virgyn	rrri

B ij

¶ Lete no man thynke foz to gather plenty,
y̆ fat .liiij. yere he haue none.
Nomoze than yf his barne wer e empty
In septembze/whan all the cozne is gone.

SEP Sentere. The nyght is .xij. houres,
and the daye is .xij. houres.

xbj f Saynt gyles abbot
b   g Saynt anthony martyz.

j

ij

	¶		ij
xiij	b	translacyon of s. Cuthberte	iiij
ij	c	Bertyne abbotte	v
	d	saynt Eugenius	vj
x	e		vij
	f	[ ]	viij
xviij	g	saynt gorgone martyr	ix
vij	¶	saynt sylueus bysshoppe	x
	b		xj
xv	c	saynt marciane bysshoppe	xij
iiij	d	saynt Maurilius bysshoppe	xiij
	e	[ ]	xiiij
xij	f	¶ [ ]	xv
j	g	saynt Edyth virgyn.	xvj
	¶	saynt Lamberte bysshoppe	xvij
ix	b	saynt victor and corona	xviij
	c	saynt Januaryus martyr	xix
xvij	d	Saynt eustace. Vigyll	xx
vj	e	[ ]	xxj
	f	saynt mauryce and his company	xxij
xiiij	g	saynt Teclea virgyn	xxiij
iij	¶	saynt andoche martyr	xxiiij
	b		xxv
xj	c	saynt Cypryane and Justyne	xxvj
xix	d	Saynt Cosme and Dampane	xxvij
	e		xxviij
viij	f	[ ]	xxix
	g	saynt Hierome prest	xxx

By Octobze betokeneth.lr.yere.
That aege haftely doothe man affayle.
Yf he haue ought/than it dooth appere.
To lyue quyetly after his trauayle.

Octobze.The nyght is.riij.houre
and the daye is.r.houreg.

rbi   saynt Remyge byfhoppe
b   b saynt Leodegary martyz

rliij	c	saynt candidi martyr.	iij
ij	d	saynt fraunceys confessour	iiij
r	e	saynt Appolynaris martyr	v
	f	saynt fayth	vj
	g	Merci and merciliani	vij
rviij	☞	saynt Pelagie	viij
vij	b	saynt Dionysij rustici and eleutheri	ir
	c	saynt Gereon and victor	r
rv	d	saynt Nichasius bysshoppe	rj
iiij	e	saynt wylfryde	rij
	f	Transl. of saynt Edwarde	riij
rij	g	saynt Calyrte bysshop of Rome	riiij
i	☞	saynt wlfrane bysshoppe	rv
	b	Cryselonne in templo.	rvj
ir	c	saynt Audry virgyn	rvij
	d	Luke Euangelist.	rviij
rvij	e	saynt Frydeswyde virgyn	rir
vi	f	saynt Austrebert virgyn	rr
	g	saynt vrsule/with.ri.M.virgyns	rri
rliij	☞	Mary salome	rrij
ij	b	saynt Romayne bysshop.	rriij
	c	Saynt Magloze bysshoppe.	rriiij
ri	d	Crispyne and cryspyniany	rrv
rir	e	Saynt Euaryste bysshop of Rome	rrvj
	f	Uigyll.	rrvij
viij	g	Symon and Iude apostles.	rrviij
	☞	Saynt Narciscus bysshoppe.	rrir
rvi	b	Saynt germayne capua.	rrr
v	c	Saynt Quyntyne Uigyll.	rrri

B iiij

NOVEMBER.

Whan man is at.lxvj.yere olde
whyche lykened is to bareyne Nouembre
He wereth vnweldy/sekely/and colde
Than is soule helth is tyme to remembre

Nouembre. The nyght hath hou
res/and the daye is .viij. houres.
The feast of all saynes
The feast of all soules.

ij	f	saynt wenefrede virgyn.	iij
	g	saynt amantyus	iiij
r		saynt Lete preste	b
	b	saynt Leonarde	bj
rbiij	c	saynt wylfryde archbysshoppe	bij
bij	d	Quatuor coronatorum.	biij
	e	saynt theodore.	ir
rb	f	saynt Martyn bysshop of Rome	r
iiij	g	Saynt Martyn bysshop.	rj
		saynt Paterne martyr.	rij
rij	b	saynt Bryce bysshop and cofessour.	riij
i	c	Translacyon of saynt erkenwalde	riiij
	d	The sonne in Sagittarius	rb
ir	e	Saynt Edmunde archbysshoppe	rbj
	f	saynt Hewe bysshoppe.	rbij
rbij	g	octa. of saynt Martyn.	rbiij
bj		saynt Elizabeth	rir
	b	saynt Edmunde kynge	rr
riiij	c	Presentacyon of our Lady.	rrj
iij	d	saynt Cecyly virgyn and martir	rrij
	e	saynt Clement bysshop of rome	rriij
rj	f	saynt Grysogony martyr	rriiij
rir	g	saynt Katheryne virgyn.	rrb
		saynt Lini bysshoppe of Rome	rrbj
biij	b	saynt Agricole and vital.	rrbij
	c	saynt rufe martyr.	rrbiij
rbj	d	saynt saturne Vigyll.	rrir
b	e	Andrewe apostle.	rrr

The yere by Decembre taketh his ende
And so dooth man/at thre score and twelue.
Nature with aege wyll hym on message sede
The tyme is come/that he must go hym selue.

Decebre. the nyght is .xviii. houres
and the daye is .vi. houres

f ſaynt Loye byſſhoppe

xiij g ſaynt lybane

Decembre

kl	A	depoſicyon of ſaynt oſmunde	iij
r	b	ſaynt Barbara virgyn	iiij
	c	ſaynt Sabba abbot	v
rviij	d	Nicholas byſſhoppe	vj
vij	e	octaues of ſaynt andrewe	vij
	f	Concepcyon of our lady	viij
rv	g	ſaynt Cyprian abbot	ir
iiij	A	ſaynt Eulalie	r
	b	Damaſe byſſhoppe of Rome	rj
rij	c	The Sonne in Capricorne	rij
i	d	ſaynt lucy vyrgyn	riij
	e	othilie virgyn	riiij
ir	f	ſaynt valery byſſhoppe	rv
	g	O ſapiencia	rvj
rvij	A	ſaynt lazarus byſſhoppe	rvij
vi	b	ſaynt Gratian byſſhoppe	rviij
	c	ſaynt venyce virgyn	rir
riiij	d	ſaynt Iulyan martyr	rr
iij	e	Saynt Thomas Apoſtle	rri
	f	rrr. martyrs	rrij
ri	g	vyctory virgyn	rriij
rir	A	Vigyll	rriiij
	b	Nacyvyte of our lorde	rrv
viij	c	Steuen prothomartyr	rrvj
	d	Iohan euangeliſt	rrvij
rvi	e	Childermas daye	rrviij
v	f	Thomas martyr	rrir
	g	Tranſlacyon of ſaynt James	rrr
riij	A	ſaynt Sylueſter byſſhop of Rome	rrri

¶ Note the golden nombre that is writen after
the sayntes on the ryght hande in the moneth of
Marche and Apryll. And the sonday nexte after
the golde nōbre for the yeare shall be Ester day

¶ The dayes of the weke Multiplied.

¶ Sonday.

I Am Sonday mooste honorable
The heed of al the weke dayes
That day all thynges laborable
Ought for to reste/& gyue prayse
To our Creatour/that alwayes
wolde haue vs reste after trauayle
Man/seruaunt/and thy beaste he sayes
And the other to thyne auayle.

¶ Monday.

¶ Monday men ought me for to call.
In whiche good workes ought to begynne
~~the seconde dede of all~~
Intendynge for to flee deedly synne
This worldly goodes truely to vynne
with labour/and true exercyse
For who of good workes can not blynne
To his rewarde/shall vynne Paradyse.

¶ Tuesday.

¶ I tuesday am also named of Mars
Called of goddes armypotent
I loue neuer for to be scars
Of workes/but alwayes dylygent
Strvynge agaynste lyfe indigent
Beynge in this worlde/or elles where

To serue our lorde/with good intent
As of duety/we are bounde here.

℥ Wednesday.

℥ Wednesday/sothely is my name
Amydes the weke is my beynge
Wherin all vertues dothe frame
By the meanes of good lyuynge
I do remembre the heuenly kynge
That was solde in my season
I do worke with true meanynge
Hym for to serue/as it is reason

℥ Thursday.

℥ I am the meryest of seuen
Called thursday verely
In my tyme the kynge of heuen
Made his souper merely
~~In forme of breade~~/gaue his body
To his Apostles/as it is playne
And then washed theyr fete mekely
And went to Olyuet mountayne

℥ Fryday.

℥ Named I am deuoute fryday.
The whiche careth for no delyte
But to mourne/fast/deale and pray
I do set all my hole appetyte
To thynke on the Jues dyspyte
Howe they dyd Chryste on the tre rent
And thynkynge howe I may be quyte
At the dredefull Iudgement

℥ Saterday.

Saterday I am comynge laste
Trustynge on the tyme well spent
Hauynge euer mynde stedfaste
On that lorde that harowed hell
That he my synnes wyll expell
At the instaunce of his Mother
whose goodnesse dothe farre excell
whome I serue aboue all other amen.

¶The commaundementes of God gyuen by
Moyses/and expounded by Chryst vnto our
Mother tongue/very necessarye and ex=
pedyent for youthe and all other for
to lerne and to knowe.

¶The fyrste Table.

Am the Lorde thy god/why
che haue brought the out
of the lande of Egypt and
out of the house of bondage
Exodi.xx. Thou shalte ha
ue none other goddes i my
syght. Deuter.vj. Thou
shalte make the no graue
ymage:neyther any simi=
litude that is i heue aboue
or in the earthe beneathe/or in the water that is
beneath the earthe. Se that thou neyther bowe
thy selfe to them:neyther serue them. For I the
lorde thy god am a gelouse god/& vysite the syn=
ne of the fathers vpon the chyldre vnto the thyrde
and fourth generacyon of them that hate me/and

yet shewe mercye to thousandes amõge thē that
loue me and kepe my commaundementes.

Exo.ir. Deute.vi. Math.rii. Heare Israell/our
lorde god is one lorde : and thou shalt loue thy
lorde god with all thy herte / with all thy Sou-
le/with all thy mynde/and with all thy strength.
Thou shalte worshyp thy lorde god/& hym onely
shalte thou serue.

C The .X. commaundement.

Thou shalt not take the name of the lorde
thy god in vayne. For the Lorde wyll not
holde hym gyltlesse/that taketh the name of the
lorde his god in vayne.   Mathew.v.

Ye haue herde howe it was sayde to thē of olde
tyme.Thou shalt not forsweare thy selfe / but
shalte performe thyn othes to the Lorde.
I say vnto you/sweare not at all:neyther by he-
uē/for it is goddes seate/nor by the earth/for it is
his fote stole/neyther by Jerusalē/for it is the Ci-
tye of þ great kynge.Neyther shalt thou sweare
by thy heade : bycause thou canst not make one
whyte heare or a blacke. But let your communi-
cacyon be:yea/yea & nay nay: for what socuer is
more then that/commeth of euyll.

C The .X. commaundement.

Remembre the Sabbath daye that thou
sanctify it. Exodi.rr. Syxe dayes mayste
thou labour/and do all that thou hast to do / but
the seuenth daye is the Sabbath of the Lorde
thy god. In it thou shalte do no maner worke/

neyther thou / noz thy sone / noz thy doughter
neyther thy manseruaunt / noz thy mayde seruaunt / noz thy catell: noz yet the straunger that
is within thy gates. Foz in syxe dayes the Lozde
made heuen and earth / and the see / and all that
is in them / and rested the seuenth day wherfoze
the Lozde blessed the seuenth daye / & halowed it
Math·xij·Mark·ij· It is lefull to do a good dede
on the Sabbath day. Foz the sone of mã is lozde
euen of the Sabbath day. The Lozde sayth by
his prophet. Esay·xxvi·Ihon· That his sabbath
is halowed and kepte / when we rest and cease to
do our owne wyll / to folowe oure owne wayes / &
to speake our owne wozdes: when we in wozde /
thought / and dede fulfyll his well (I say) & not
ours: and when we suffer hym to do his wozkes
in vs / that at the last / we may come to that Sabbath and true reste / euen eternall lyfe / whiche
Chzyst the Lozde of the sabbath hath opteyned
foz vs by his blode.

The seconde Table.
The·v·commaundement

Honoure thy Father and thy Mother / that
thy dayes may be longe in the lande whiche the lozde thy god gyueth the. Exod·xx
Honour thy father and thy mother. Ephe·vi
Coll·iij· Honour father and mother: this is the
fyzste commaundement that hath any promyse
that thou mayst be in good estate: and lyue longe
on the earthe. By this commaundement Chzyste

teacheth vs not onely to haue our father and
mother in reuerence / and to obey them / as he
hym selfe was subiecte vnto his Mother the
virgyn Mary: but also to mynyster vnto theyr ne
cessytes. Math. ꝑe a͑

℃ The X. cōmaundement.

Thou shalt not kyll. Matth. v. ye haue
herde how it was sayde vnto them of the
olde tyme. Thou shalt not kyll. who soeuer kyll
leth shalbe in daunger of iudgement. But J say
to you: who soeuer is angry with his brother
shalbe in daunger of iudgement. who soeuer
sayth to his brother / Racha: shalbe in daunger
of a counsell. But who soeuer sayth: thou fole
shalbe in daunger of hell fyer. ye haue
herde howe it is sayd. Thou shalte loue thy
neyghbour: and hathe thyn enemye. But J say
vnto you / loue your enemyes / blysse them that
curse you / do good to them that hathe you pray
for them that do you wronge and persecute you:
that ye may be the chyldrē of your father whiche
is in heuen. For he maketh the sonne to ary=
se on the euyll and on the good: and sendeth his
rayne on the iuste and on the vniuste.

℃ The X. cōmaundement.

Thou shalt not breake wedlocke. Math. v
ye haue herde how it was sayd to them
of olde tyme / thou shalte not commyt aduoutry.
But J say to you / that who soeuer loketh on a
wyfe / lustynge after her / hath cōmytted aduou=

℃

try with her all redy in his herte. ☙☙☙ Let
wedlocke be had in pꝛyce in all poyntes/and let
thy chambꝛe be vndefyled/foꝛ hooꝛe kepers and
aduouterers God wyll iudge.

C The .ix. commaundemente.

☙ Hou shalt not steale. ☙☙☙☙☙

☙ Steale not:defraude no man. yf any man
wyll sue the at the lawe / and take thy cote
from the : let hym haue thy cloke also : gyue to
hym that asketh : and from hym that wolde bo=
rowe:turne not awaye. ☙☙☙ Now is the=
re vtterlye a faute amonge you:because ye go to
lawe one with another? Why rather suffre ye
not wꝛonge?why rather suffre ye not your selues
to be robbed?yea / euen youre selues do wꝛonge
and robbe/and that the bꝛethꝛene. Ephesi. iiij.
Let hym that dyd steale / steale no moꝛe / but let
him rather labour with his handes some good
thynge / that he maye haue to gyue vnto hym
that nedeth.

C The .X. commaundemente.

☙ Hou shalte beare no false wytnesse a=
gaynst thy neyghbour. ☙☙☙☙☙
Beare no false wytnesse I say to you / that of
euery ydle woꝛde whiche men shal haue spoken
they shal gyue accomptes at the daye of iudge=
ment. ☙☙☙ Wherfoꝛe put away lyng / and
speake euery man trueth to his neyghboure /
foꝛ as moche as we are membꝛes one of ano=
ther. Let not fylth communycacyon pꝛocede out

of your mouthes : but that whiche is good to
edifye with al / when nede is / that it may haue
fauour with the hearers. Ephe. v. Let al bytter=
nesse/fearfnesse and wrath / rozynge and curfed
speakyng / be put away from you. Let no fylthy=
nesse/folysshe talkyng / noz iestynge (whiche are
not comly) be ones named amonge you: but ra=
ther gyuyng of thankes.

℟ The x. commaundement

x. Thou shalt not coueyt thy neyghboures
house. Neyther shalt thou coueyt thy
neyghbours wyfe: his man seruaunt/his mayde
his oxe / his asse / oz ought that is his.

What foeuer
ye wolde that men shulde do to you : euen so doo
ye to them. To loue a mannes neyghbour as
hym felfe / is a greater thynge then all burnte
offerynges and facryfyces. Be not ouercomme
with lufte/foz the care of this worlde and the di=
fceptfulnesse of ryches choke te worlde.

Let your conuerfacyon
bet without couetoufnes / and be content with
that that ye haue al redy. Godlynes is great
ryches / yf a man be content with that he hath.
Foz we brought nothynge in to the worlde/and
it is a playne cafe/that we cary nothyng out.
When we haue fode and rapment/let vs ther
with be content. They that wyll be ryche/fall
in to temptacyon and fnares / and in to many
folysshe and noyfom luftes/whiche drowne men

in perdicyon and deſtruccion. For couetouſnes
is the rote of all euyl: whiche whyle ſome luſted
after/ they erred from the fayth/ and tangled the
ſelues with many ſorowes.

Theſe wordes which I cōmaunde the this day
ſhall be in thyne herte/ and thou ſhalt whette
them on thy chyldzen/ and ſhalt talke of them
when thou arte at home in thy houſe/ and as
thou walkeſt by the way/ and when thou lyeſt
downe/ and when thou ryſeſt vp: and thou ſhalte
bynde them for a ſygne vpon thy hande. And
they ſhall be papers of remembraunce bytwene
thyne eyes/ and thou ſhalte wryte them vpon
the poſtes of thy houſe/ and vpon thy gates.

Take hede and heare al theſe wodes
which I commaunde the/ that it may go wel
with the/ and with thy chyldzen after the for
euer/ when thou doeſt that whiche is good and
ryght in the ſyght of the lorde thy god.

Se thou do that whiche is ryght in
the ſyght of the lord/ that thou mayſt proſper.

Ye ſhall do after nothynge that we
do here this day/ euery man what ſemeth hym
good in his owne eyes. But what ſoeuer I com:
maunde you/ that take hede ye do/ and put no:
thynge therto/ nor take ought therfrom.

Curſed be he that contynueth not
in all the wordes of this lawe/ to do them.

Yf ye loue me/ kepe my commaundemē:
tes. Happy are they that heare the

worde of god/and kepe it. who soeuer
shall kepe the hole lawe/and yet fayle in one
poynt/he is gylty in al. For he that sayd. Thou
shalt not commyt aduoutry: sayd also: thou shalt
not kyll. They that feare the lorde kepe
his commaundementes.

℄ The symbole or Crede of the greate Doctour
Athanasius bysshoper in the churche.

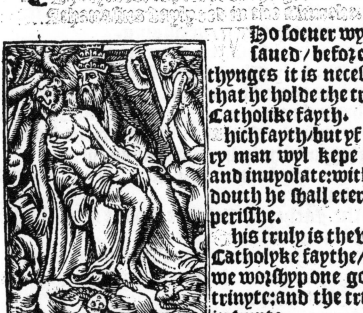

Ho soeuer wyll be
saued/before all
thynges it is necessary
that he holde the trewe
Catholike fayth.

hich fayth/but yf eue=
ry man wyl kepe hole
and inuyolate: without
douth he shall eternaly
perisshe.

his truly is the verye
Catholyke faythe/that
we worshyp one god in
trinyte: and the trinyte
in vnyte.

Neyther confoundyng the persones: neyther se=
peratynge the substance.

The persone of the Father is one/the person
of the Sone an other/the person of the holye
Ghoste an other.

But of the Father/of the Sone/and of the ho:

C iij

ly Ghost/there is one dyuinyte/equal glozy coe=
ternall maiesty e.

Such as is the Father/suche is the Sonne su=
che is the holy Ghoste.

The Father is vncreate/the Sone vncreat/the
holy Ghost is vncreat.

The father is without measure/the Son with
out measure/the holy ghost without measure.

The Father is euerlastynge/the Sone euerla=
styng/the holy Ghost euerlasting.

And not withstandyng there be not.iij.euerla=
styng/the holy Ghost euerlastyng.

Euyn as there be not thze vncreat:noz.iij. vn=
mesurate/but one vncreat / et one vnmesurate.

Lykewyse the Father is almyghty/the Son al=
myghty,and the holy Ghoste almyghty.

And yet they bet not thze Almyghtyes/but one
god almyghty.

So the Father is God/the Sonne God/the ho=
ly ghost is God.

And yet they be not.iij goddes/but one god.

So the Father is a lozde/the Sone a lozde / the
holy Ghost a lozde.

And yet they be not.iij.lozdes/but one lozde.

Foz as we be compelled by the Chzistian veryte
to confesse seperatly euery one person to be God
and Lozde.

So are we prohybite by the Catholike relygyon
of Chzistes fayth to say that there be.iij.Goddes
oz thze lozdes.

The Father is made of none : neyther created no2 gotten.

The Sone is fro the Father alone: neyther made ne create/but gotten.

The holy Ghost is fro the Father/and the Sone/neyther made created/no2 gotten but procedynge.

And so there is but one Father/not th2e Fathers/one Sonne/not th2e Sonnes/one holy Ghost:/not th2e holy Ghostes.

And in this Trinyte/there is none befo2e o2 after another/nothynge mo2e o2 lesse: but all the th2e persons be coeterne/and coequall to them selte.

So that by alwayes as now it hath ben aboue sayd/the Trinyte in vnite/and the vnite in Trinyte may be wo2sthypped.

He therfo2e that wyll be saued/let hym vnderstande thus of the Trinyte.

But it is necessary vnto euerlastyng health/that euery ch2istian beleue also faythfully the incarnacyon of our lo2de Jesu ch2yste.

It is therfo2e the ryght fayth:that we beleue & confesse that our lo2de Jesu Ch2yste the Sone of God/is God and man.

He is god by the substance of the Father gotten befo2e all wo2ldes/and he is man by the substance of his mother:bo2ne in the wo2lde.

Perfyte God : perfyte man : beynge of a soule

The symbole of Athanasius reasonable/and of fleshe humayne.

Equall to the Father by his Godhed/lesse the the Father by his manhed.

Whiche thoughe he be God and man/yet is there not twayne but one Chryste.

Truely he is one not by turnyng of his godhed in to māhed/but by assumptynge of his manhed in to godhed.

Beynge one to all intentes / not by confusion of substance/but by vnite of person.

For as the reasonable soule and the fleshely body is or maketh one man / so God and man is one Chryste.

Whiche suffered death for our saluacyon/descended to helle/and rose from death the thyrde daye.

Whiche ascended to heuens / sytteth at the ryght hāde of God the Father almyghty from thense shall he come to Iudge the quycke and dead.

At whose comynge all men muste ryse wt theyr bodyes / and shall gyue accompt of theyr owne propre dedes.

And they that haue done well shall go in to euerlastyng lyfe / they that haue done euyll in to euerlastynge fyre.

This in the Catholyke fayth / whiche excepte euery man faythfully and stedfastly do beleue he can not be saued.

Bysshop muste be fautlesse, the husbande of one wyfe: sober discrete: honestly appareled: herberous: apte to teache: not dronken: no fyghter: not gyuen to fylthy lucre: but gentyll: abhorrynge fyghtynge: ab horrynge couetousnesse: and one that ruleth his owne house honestly / hauynge chyldren vnder obedyence / with all honeste.

Ye that are rulers of the earth / se that you loue ryghteousnes / and that you commyt none vnryghteousnes in iudgement. Thou shalte not fauour the poore / nor honoure the myghty: but shalt iudge thy neyghbour ryghtteously.

e shall not deceyue your brethren: neyther with weyght nor measure: but shall haue true ballances / and true weyghtes / for I am the Lor de your God.

usbandes loue your wyues euen as chryst loued the congregacyon / and gaue hym selfe for it to sanctyfy it / and clensed it in the fountayne of water thorowe the worde / to make it vnto hym selfe a gloryous congregacyon without spot or wrencle / or any suche thynge. So ought men to loue theyr wyues / as theyr owne bodyes. He that loueth his wyfe / lo

neth hym self. For no man euer yet hated his ow
ne flesshe/but norysshed is. &c.

¶ Wyues. Ephe. v.

Wyues submyt your selues to your owne hus¬
bandes/as to the lorde. For the husbande is the
wyues hed/euen as Chryst is the heed of the con
gregacyon. Therfore as the congregacyon is in
subieccyon to Chryste/lykewyse lette the wyues
be in subieccyon to theyr husbandes in all thyn¬
ges.

¶ Fathers and mothers. Ephe. vi.

Ye fathers moue not your chyldren vnto wrath
but brynge them vp with the nurture and infor¬
macyon of the lorde.

¶ Chyldren. Ephe. vi.

Chyldren obey your fathers and mothers in
the Lorde: for so it is ryght. Honour thy father
and mother (that is the fyrst commaundement
that hathe any promyse) that thou mayste be in
good estate and lyue longe on the earthe.

¶ Maysters. Collo. iii.

Ye maysters do to youre seruauntes that whiche
is iuste and equall/puttynge away all bytternes
se and theatenynges/knowynge that euen ye
also haue a mayster in heuen.

¶ Seruauntes. Collo. iii.

Seruauntes/be obedyent to youre bodyly
maysters in all thynges: not with eye seruice as
mē pleasers/but i synglenesse of herte/tearynge
god. And what soeuer ye do/do it hertely as
thoughe ye dyd it vnto the lorde/and not vnto

The preface & the maner to lyue well.
men:for as moche as ye knowe that of the lorde
ye shall receyue the rewarde of inheritaunce for
ye serue the Lorde Chrift.

Wydowes. i. Timoth. v.

She that is a very wydowe and frendlesse: put=
teth her truste in god/and contynueth in supply=
cacyon and prayer nyght and day.

The somme of all.

Loue thy neyghbour as thy felf.& what foe=
uer ye wolde ȳ other fhulde do to you do you
eue ȳ fame to thē/and what ye wolde not ȳ other
men fhulde do to you/fe ȳ ye do it not to them.

The preface & ȳ maner to lyue well/deuoutlye
falutarly euery day for all perfones of meane esta=
te. Cōppyled by mayster Johan quētin doctour in
dyuinyte at Parys: tranflated out of frenche in
to englyffhe by Robert Coplād prynter at Lōdō

FOr to begyn

the maner of falutary or helth full
lyuyng. And to come to perfection
(how well I haue more nede to be instruct than
for to teche other) yet kepe thefe fmall doctrines
here folowyng to your powers. Fyrst ryfe vp at
vj. of the clocke in the mornynge in all feafons
and in your ryfyng do as foloweth. Thanke our
lorde of reft that he gaue you that nyght.
Commende you to god/bleffed lady faynt ma=
ry/and to that faynt whiche is feafted that day/

~~and to all the faynts of heuen~~ Secōdly befeche
god that he pꝛeferue the that day/frō deedly fyn
ne/& at all other tymes. And pꝛay hym that all
the werkes that other dooth foꝛ you may be ac=
cept to the lawde of his name/of his gloꝛioꝰ mo
ther/& of all the company of heuen. ¶Whan
hye haue arayed you/fay in your chambꝛe oꝛ lod=
gyng:matyns/pꝛyme & houres yf ye may. Than
go to the chyꝛche oꝛ ye do ony woꝛldly werkes yf
ye haue no nedefull befyneffe & abyde in the chyꝛ
che the fpace ~~of the two maffe whyle~~ where ye
fhall thynke and thanke god of his benefytes.
Thynke a whyle on the goodneffe of god/on his
dyuyne myght and vertue. Thynke what gyft
he hath gyuen to you to create you fo nobly/as
to his ymage & lykeneffe.Thynke alfo what gra
ce he hath done to you in the facrament of bap=
tyfme/clenfyng your foule from fynne. Thynke
how many tymes ye haue offended hym fyth ye
were criftened.Thynke how mekely he hath aby
den your retournyng from fynne. Thynke from
how many daungers he hath pꝛeferued your bo
dy and foule. Thynke how yll ye haue beftowed
the tyme that he hath gyuen you to do penaunte
Thynke how many tymes he hath foꝛgyuē you
infhꝛyft/et how many tymes ye haue fallē to fyn
ne agayn. Thynke in what payne ye had bēnow
et euer yf god had taken you out of this woꝛlde
whan ye were in deedly fynne. Thynke how de=
rely he bought you frō the daunger of the deuyll

The pface & the maner to lyue well
suffryng cõtynuall paynes in this worlde/about
the space of .xxxiii. yeres goynge barefote i colde &
heate/suffryng hõgre/& thyrst/& many shamefull
iniuryes & how derely he redemed you gyuyng his
precious body/his blod/& his soule.& at this point
cõsydre all the paynes of his wofull passyon / as
god wyll gyue you grace Thynke also what pay
ne his dere & gloryous mother suffred all ý why
le.Consydre his sharpe iugement at the houre of
dethe.And touchyng this dethe thynke often the
ron/and that ye can not escape it / nor knoweth
whan / nor how , in what estate:nor what place
nor tyme day:nor houre. Thynke thã what shall
become of the worldly goodes that ye haue ga
dred & spared with grete labour & how lothe ye
shall be to leaue thẽ and all your frendes & kyns
folke.An ý more is whã your soule i grete payne
shall leaue your body to rotte in the erthe . Con
sydre thã what shall become of your strenght:be
aute/youthe helthe & other welthe of the body.
Thynke what the poore soule shall do whan it
goothalone without company where it was ne
uer Thynke what it shall do whã it seeth the hor
ryble enemyes that wolde drawe it to pdicyon yf
ye deye in deedly synne . Thynke how wofull a
iourney it shall be whan ye must yelde a generall
rekenyng of all your werkes/wordes/& though
tes without excepcyõ of ony thyng Thynke how
god shall iuue you grace. Thynke on ý horryble
paynes of hell/& on the cruell cpany of deuylles:

The preface of the maner to lyue well,
where without ende ye shall neuer / haue releas
yf ye deye in deedly synne. And thynke on the ine
stimable ioye of the sayntes i heuē / ꝑ w iche our
lorde hath promised you yf ye lyue out of deedly
synne: et loue hym aboue all thyng. And haue ye
a pfyte hope yf ye lyue wel ye shall come to that
glory. Amē. ¶ And theſſ ben the thoughtes that
I wyll that ye haue in the chyrche.

¶ And yf by ony other reasonable besynesse ye
may not be so long in the chyrche / at is it sayd he
re afore, yelde thankes to god of his goodnesse.
And thynke on the resydew in your hows ones in
the day or in the nyght yf ye may.

¶ Whā ye are cōe fro ꝑ chyrch take hede to your
housholde or occupacyō tyll dyner tyme. And in
so doyng thynke sōtyme that ꝑ payne ꝑ ye suffre
in this worlde is nothyng to the regarde of ꝑ in
fynite glory ꝑ ye shall haue yf ye take it mekely.
Thā take your refecciō or mele reasonably wout
ercesse or ouer moche for beryng of your meate
for there is as moche daunger i to lytell as in to
moche yf ye fast ones in a weke it is ynought / be
syde vigilles & ymbre dayes out of lenten. And yf
ye tynke ꝑ fastyng be not good nor pfytable do
by counsell Rest you after dyner an houre or half
an houre as ye thynke best / prayeng god that in
that rest he wyll accept your helthe / to ꝑ ende ꝑ
after it ye may serue hym ꝑ more deuoutly. The
resydew of ꝑ day bestowe i your besynnesse to the
pleasure of god. As touchyn your seruyce say vn

to tiers afore dyner. and make an ende of all be
fore souper. And whan ye may / ~~say dyrige. and
comendacyons for all chrysted soules at the lecst
way on the holy dayes and yf ye haue leaser say
them on other dayes. at the leest with thre lessos~~
~~Shryue you euery weke to your curate except ye
haue grete lette. and beware ye passe not a four~
tenyght excepte verray grete lette.~~ Yf ye be of
power refuse not your almesse to the fyrst poore
body that axeth it of you that day. yf ye thynke
it nedefull. Take payne to here & kepe the worde
of god. Confesse you euery day to god without fay
le / of suche synnes as ye knowe that ye haue do=
ne that day. Consydre ofte eyther by day or nyght
whan ye do awake what our lorde dyde at that
houre the day of his blyssed passyon / & whete he
was at that houre. Seke a god & fayth full fre
de of god conuersacyon to whome ye may dyscouer
your mynde secretes Enqre & proue hym well or
ye trust i hym. And wha ye haue well pued hym
do all by is counsell. Day lytell / & folowe vtuous
copany. Eschew ye felaw shyppe of them ye wol
de not be lyke. After all werke praysc & take god /
loue hi aboue all thynges / & serue hym & his glo=
rious moder diligetely. do to nouer ther but that
ye wolde were done to you loue the welth of ano=
ther as your owne. And in goyng to your bedde
haue sbe good tought eyther of the passys of our
lord / or of you sines / or of ye paynes ye soules haue
purgatory. or sbe other good spirituall toughtes

And than I hope your lyuyng shall be accepta=
ble and pleasyng to god.

¶ Here foloweth a very be houesull techyng a
remedy for euery man/and woman dasyly to co=
me out of synne & to come soone in to the state of
helth after the doctryne of mayster Johan gersō
chaunceler of Parys/and doctour in dyuynite.

God our souerain lorde knowlegyng
the grete fragilites inclinacyō of our
synne:is alway red of his infynyte py
te and goodnesse to do vs mercy and
foꝛgyuenesse so that truly:without
faynyng:with a good hert and contrite thought
we offre and say the thre verytees folowyng.

¶ The fyꝛst verite.

My god I knowlege and confesse to haue offen
ded & synned agaynst thy goodnesse:bꝛekyng thy
commaundementes in suche maner and suche.

Here ought the persone to espyꝛe thre syꝛtes dotte:
particulyer and general:beyng soꝛy:& thynke on
them.Of the which synnes I am soꝛy:and repēt
me foꝛ the honour of the that arte all good/onely
woꝛthy to be serued/obeyed/honoured & woꝛshyp
ped.   ¶ The seconde veryte.

Good loꝛde I haue good purpose by your helpe
to kepe me from hens foꝛwarde to offende you
without bꝛekyng your commaundementes/and
to fle & eschewe to my power all occasyōs of synne.

¶ The thyꝛde veryte

Lord god I haue good and stedfast wyl to be confessed clerely of all my synnes/in tyme and place after the commaundement of you/and our holy chyrche/or at suche a feest/or suche after your ordinaunce and commaundemēt of our other/holy chyrche/and to make satiffaction to you/and to my neyghbour.

Corpora sanctorum in pace sepulta sunt/et viuent nomina eorum in eternum. Letamini in domino et exultate iusti. Et gloriamini omnes recti corde. Oremus.

Propiciare nobis domine famulis tuis per sanctorum tuorum (quorum reliquie in presenti requiescunt ecclesia) merita gloriosa: vt eorum pia intercessione ab omnibus semper protegamur aduersis. Per dominum. Oratio.

Sancte dei genitricis marie semper virginis gloriose/et beatarum omnium celestium virtutum/sanctorumque patriarcharum/prophetarum/apostolorum/martyrum/confessorum/virginum/atque omnium sanctorum tuorum: quesumus omnipotens deus meritis et precibus placatus nobis misericordiam tuam/et da populo inuiolabilem fidei firmitatem & pacem: repelle a nobis hostem/famem/et pestem/et omnem immundiciam: da nobis in tua virtute constantiam et fortitudinem: immitte hostibus nostris formidinem et inualitudinem: retribue omnibus nobis bona facientibus bona vite eterne beatitudinem: da inimicis nostris

D i

et perſequentibus nos recognitionem et indul=
gentiam:concede defunctis noſtris et omnibus
in chꝛiſto quieſcentibusremiſſionem peccatoꝛum
et requiem ſempiternam.Per eundem dominū.

Anima chꝛiſti ſanctifica me/coꝛp9 chꝛiſti
ſalua me:ſāguis chꝛiſti inebꝛia me:aqua
lateris chꝛiſti laua me: paſſio chꝛiſti ꜩfoꝛ
ta me:ſudoꝛ vult9chꝛiſti virtuoſiſſime ſa
na me.O bone ieſu exaudi me:ꬠ ne pmittas me
ſeparari a te.Ab hoſte maligno defende me:in ho
ra moꝛtis voca me/ꬠ pone me iurta te:vt cum an
gelis et ſanctis tuis laudem te dominum ſalua=
toꝛem meum in ſecula ſeculoꝛum.Amen.

An other pꝛayer at the eleuacyon.

Ue domine ieſu chꝛiſte verbum patris/fi=
lius virginis/agnus dei/ſalus mundi/ho=
ſtia ſacra/vera caro/fons pietatis.
ue domine ieſu chꝛiſte laus angeloꝛum/gloꝛia
ſanctoꝛum/viſio pacis/deitas integra/verus ho=
mo/flos ꬠ fructus virginis matris.
ue domine ieſu chꝛiſte ſplendoꝛ patris / pꝛin=
ceps pacis/ianua regni/panis biu9/virginis par
tus/vas deitatis.
ue domine ieſu chꝛiſte lumen celi/pꝛeciū mun
di:gaudium noſtrum/angeloꝛum panis/iubilus
coꝛdis:rex et ſponſus virginitatis.
ue dñe ieſu xpe via dulcis / veritas vera/pꝛe=
miū noſtrū/charitas ſumma/fons amoꝛis/pax ꬠ
dulcedo/requies vera/et vita perennis.Amen.

¶A prayer to our lozde.

Slue sancta caro dei:per quā salui fiunt rei
seruos tuos redemisti:dū in cruce pependi=
sti:quādo moztē occidisti. Vnda q̄ de te manauit:
a peccato nos mundauit/q̄ d patrauit pzimus hō
inobediēs de pomo. Sctā caro tu me munda:san
guis z benigna vnda/laua me ab omī lozde/z ab
infernali mozte.Per tuā benignitatē:cōfer michi
sanitatē:et sanctam pzosperitatē. Frange meos
inimicos:fac eos michi amicos:et superbiā illozū
destrue rex angeloz.Tu qui es salutis poztus:pz=
sta michi tuū cozpʒ/ī exitu mee moztis Libera me
dezfoztis a leone rugiēte dzachoncʒ furiēte. Da
michi fidē iustoz/q̄ regnas in perpetuum.Amen.

¶Whan thou goest to receyue
the body of our lozde/say.

Domine non sum dignʒ vt intres sub tectū
meū:sed tu domine q̄ dixisti/qui manducāt
meam carnem et bibit meum sanguinē in me ma
net et ego ī eo:pzopitius esto michi peccatozi per
sumptionem cozpozis et sanguinis tui: et pzesta
vt nō ad iudiciū damnationis illud sumā:sed mi=
sericozdia tua pzeueniēte in salutē et remissionē
peccatozū meozum.Qui cum patre et spiritu san
cto viuis et regnas dcus.Per omnia secula secu=
rum.Amen. ¶Whan thou hast receyued.
D ij

Era perceptio corporis et sanguinis tui ol:
potens deus non veniat michi ad iudiciuz
neꝗ ad cōdēnationē:ſed ſit oim pctōꝝ meoꝝ optā
ta remiſſio/aſe ⁊ corporis pia gubernatio/et po:
tens ad vitā pꝛeſentē ⁊ eternā introductio. Qui
cū pꝛe et ſpiritu ſancto viuis ⁊ regnas dc⁹. Per.

The Golpell of ſaynt Johan.i.

IN ẏ begynnig
was the woꝛde
And the woꝛde
was with god
And ẏ woꝛd was with
god. The ſame wasin ẏ
begynnig with god. Al
thynges were made by
it/and without it was
made nothynge. That
was made in it was lyfe
⁊ the lyfe wasthe lyght
of men/⁊ the lyght ſhy:
neth in ẏ darkenes/but
the darkenes compꝛehē
ded it not. There was a man ſent frō god/whoſe
name was Johan. The ſame came as a wytneſſe
to beare wytneſſe of the lyght/that all men
through hym myght beleue. He was not that
lyght/but to beare wytneſſe of the lyght. That
was a true lyght/whiche lyghteth all men that
come in to the woꝛlde. He was i the woꝛlde/and
the woꝛlde was made by hym:and yet the woꝛlde
knewe hym not. He came amonge his owne/and

His owne receyued hym not. But as many as re=
ceyued hym/to them gaue he power to be the so=
nes of god/in that they beleue on his name/whi=
che were borne not of bloude nor of the wyll of
the flesshe/nor yet of the wyll of man/but of god.
And the worde was made flesshe/& dwelt among
vs. And we saw the glory of it as the glory of the
onely begotten sonne of the father: whiche worde
was full of grace and verite. Antheme.

We do call vpon the/we do worshyp the / we do
prayse the/o blyssed Trinyte.

Blessed be the lordes name all other before.

The answere. From this tyme forth and euer=
more. Let vs pray.

O God the protectour of all that truste in the/
without whome nothynge is of value / no=
thyng is holy / multiply thy mercy vpon vs that
through thy gouernaunce and guydyng we may
so passe in goddes temporall/that we lese not the
eternal. By Chryst our lorde.

The gospell of saynt Luke.

THe aungell Gabriell was
sente frome God vnto a cy=
tye of Galylee/named Na=
zareth/vnto a virgyn spou=
sed to a man / whose name was Io=
seph/of the house of Dauid: and the
virgyns name was Marye. And the
aungell wente vnto her and sayde.
hayle full of grace/the lorde is with the/blyssed
arte thou amonge all women. When she sawe

D iij

hym/she was abasshed at his sayenge / and caste
in her mynde what maner of salutacyon that
shulde be. And the aungell sayde vnto her. Fea=
re not Mary/for thou hast foũde grace with god.
Loo/thou shalte cõceyue in thy wombe/and shall
beare a Sone / and his name shall be called Je=
sus.He shalbe great / and shal be called the sone
of the hyghest.   And the lorde god shall gyue to
hym the seate of his father Dauid : and he shall
reygne ouer the house of Jacob for euer : and of
his kyngdome shall be no ende. Then sayd Ma=
ry vnto the Aungell.Howe shall this be/sayenge
J knowe not a man?And the aungell answered
and sayde vnto her. The holy ghoste shall come
vpõ the/and the power of the hyghest shall ouer=
shadowe the.Therfore that holy thynge whiche
shall be borne/shalbe called the sone of god. And
beholde thy cosyn Elizabeth.she hath also cõcey=
ued a sone in her olde age. And this is her.vi.mo
neth though she be called barayne/for with God
shall nothynge be vnpossyble. And Mary sayde.
Beholde the hande maydene of the lorde / be it
vnto me euen as thou haste sayde. Thankes be
to god.

The gospell of saynt Mathewe.
The seconde chapter.

WHen Jesus was borne in Bethleem(a
towne of Jury)whiche in tyme of Hero=
de the kynge:beholde there cam wyse men from
the East to Jerusalẽ/sayenge. Where is he that
is borne kynge of the Jewes. We haue sene his

The gospell of saynt Mathewe.

starre in the East/ & are come to worshyp hym. When Herode the kyng had herde this / he was troubled / & all Jerusalé with hym/ & he gathered all the cheyf Preestes & Scrybes of the people/ & demaūded of thē where Chryste shulde be borne They sayde vnto hym/ in Bethleem / a towne of Jewry. For thus it is wryten by the prophete. And thou Bethleē i the lande of Jewrye/ arte not the leest zcernynge the prynces of Juda. For out of the shall come a captayne/ whiche shall gouerne my people of Israel. Then Herode pryuely called the wyse men/ & dilygētly enquyred of thē the tyme of the. Starre that appered: & sente them to Bethleē/ sayēge. Go & serche ye dilygently for the chylde/ & whē ye haue foūde hi/ brynge me worde that I maye come & worshyppe hym also. When they herde the kynge they departed. And loo the Starre. whiche they sawe in the Easte wente before vntyll it came & stode ouer the place where the chylde was. Whē they sawe the Starre they were merueylous glad/ & wente in to the house & founde the chylde with Mary is mother / & knele downe & worshypped hym/ & opened theyr treasures/ & offered vnto hym gyftes. Golde/ Frankenscens/ and myrre. And after they were warned of god in a dreame/ that they shulde not go agayne to Herode/ they retourned i to theyr owne countre by another way.

D iiij

Fter that he apped vnto
the eleuē/as they sate at
meate/& cast i theyr teeth
theyr vnbelef & hardēsse
of herte/because they beleued not
theym/whiche hadde sene hym af
ter his resurreccyon. And he sayde
vnto thē. Go ye i to all the world
and preache the gospel to all crea
tures. He that beleueth & is bap:
tysed/shal be safe But he that beleueth not shall
shall be dampned. And these sygnes shall
folowe them that beleue. In my name shall they
cast out deuylles / & shall speake with newe ton:
ges/and shall kyll serpētes. And yf they drynke
any deadly thynge it shall not hurte theym.
They shall lay theyr handes on the sycke / & they
shall recouer. So the lorde Iesus after he had
spokē to them was receyue in to heuyn/and
sytteth on the ryght hāde of God. And
they went forth and preached eue:
ry where. And our lorde wrought
with them / and confyrmed
the worde with myra:
cles that folowed.

¶The passyon of our lorde Iesu.

Hē Iesus had spoken these wordes he wente forth with his discyples ouer the broke Cedron: where was a gardeyn/ī to the whiche he entred with his discyples. Iudas also: which betrayd hym/ knew the place for Iesy of tymes resorted thyther with his discyples. Iudas thē after that he had receyued a bonde of men / and mynysters of the hye preestes and pharises/came thyther with lanternes and fyerbrodes and weapons. Then Iesus knowynge all thynges that shulde come on hym/went forth and sayde vnto thē / whome seke ye? They answered hym. Iesus of Nazareth Iesus sayde vnto thē/ I am he. Iudas also whiche betrayed hym stode with hym. But as sone as he had sayd to them. I am he: they wēt backewardes and fell to the groūde. And he asked thē agayne/whome seke ye? They sayd Iesus of Nazareth. Iesus answered/I sayde vnto you/I am he. Yf ye seke me/let these go theyr way/that the sayeng myght be fulfylled/whiche he spake. Of them which thou gauest me/haue I not loste one Symon Peter hadde a swearde / and drewe it / & smote the hye preestes seruaunt / and cut of his

ryghte eare. The ſeruauntes name was Malcus
Then ſayde Jeſus vnto Peter: ſhall I not dꝛynke
of the cuppe/whiche my father hathe gyuen me.
Then the companye and the captayne / and the
mynyſters of the Jewes toke Jeſus and bounde
hym/and ledde hym awaye to Anna fyꝛſte: foꝛ he
was father law vnto Cayphas / whiche was the
hye pꝛeeſt that ſame yeare. Cayphas was he that
gaue counſell to the Jewes that it was expedyēt
that one man ſhulde dye foꝛ the people. And ſy=
mō Peter folowed Jeſus/⁊ anotherdiſcyple that
diſcyple was knowē of the hye peſtc/⁊ wēt i with
Jeſ⁹i to the palayes of the hye pꝛeeſt. But Peter
ſtode at the doꝛe without. Then went that other
diſcyple whiche was knowen vnto the hye pꝛeeſt
and ſpake to the dāſell that kepte the doꝛe / and
bꝛought in Peter. Then ſayde the damſell that
kepte the dooꝛe vnto Peter. Arte not thou one of
this mannes diſcyples? He ſayde. I am not. The
ſeruauntes and the miniſters ſtode there / and
had made a fyꝛe of cooles / foꝛ it was colde : and
they warmed them ſelfes. Peter alſo ſtode amon
ge them and warmed him ſelfe. The hye pꝛeeſtes
aſked Jeſus of his diſcyples/andof his doctryne
Jeſus anſwered hym. I ſpake openly in the
woꝛlde. I euer taught in the ſynagoge and in
the temple/whereal the Jues reſoꝛted/and in ſe=
crete haue I ſayde nothyng. Why aſkeſt thou
me? Aſke them whiche herde me/what I ſayde
vnto them. Beholde/they can tell what I ſayde.
When he had thus ſpoken/one of the miniſters

whiche ſtode by:ſmote Jeſus on the face/ſayeng
Anſwereſt thou the hye preeſt ſo. Jeſus anſwe=
red hym?Yf J haue ſpoken euyll beare wytneſſe
of the euyll. Yf J haue ſpeken well/why ſmyteſt
thou me.And Annas ſent hym bounde vnto Cay
phas the hye Preeſte. Symon Peter ſtode
and warmed hym ſelfe. And they ſayde vnto
hym.Arte thou not alſo one of his diſcyples. He
denyed it / and ſayde. J am not. One of the
ſeruauntes of the hye preeſt (his coſyn / whoſe
eare Peter ſmote of) ſayde vnto hym. Dyd not
J ſe the in the Gardeyn with hym. Peter de=
nyed it agayne / and immediatly the cocke
crewe. Then ledde they Jeſus from Cayphas
in to the halle of iudgement. Jt was in the
mornynge / and they theym ſelfes wente not
in to the iudgement halle / leſt they ſhulde
be defyled : but that they myghte eate the pa=
ſchall Lambe. Pylate then wente out vn=
to them / and ſayde. What accuſacyon bryn=
ge you agaynſte this man. They anſwered and
ſayde vnto hym.Yf he were not an euyll doer /
we wolde not haue delyuered hym vnto the.Thē
ſayde Pylate vnto them.Take ye hym/and iud=
ge hym after youre owne lawe.Then the Jewes
ſayde vnto hym. Jt is not laufull for vs to put
any man to deathe. That the wordes of Jeſus
myght be fulfylled which he ſpake ſygnyfyenge
what deathe he ſhulde dye. Then Pylate en=
tred into the iudgement hall agayne/and called

Iesꝰ and sayd vnto hym Arte thou the kynge of
the Iewes? Iesus answered. Sayest thou that
of thy selfe/oꝛ dyd other tell it the of me. Pylate
answered. Am I a Iewe. Thyne owne nacyõ and
hye Pꝛeestes haue delyuered the vnto me. What
haste thou done. Iesus answered. My kyngedo=
me is not of this woꝛlde. Yf my kyngedome were
of this woꝛlde/then wolde my mynysters surelye
fyghte / that I shulde not be delyuered vnto the
Iewes/but nowe is my kyngedome not frõ hen=
se. Pylate sayde vnto hi. Arte thou a kynge thẽ.
Iesus answered. Thou sayest that I am a kynge
Foꝛ this cause was I boꝛne/& foꝛ this cause came
I i to the woꝛld/that I shuld beare wytnesse vn
to the trueth. And al that are of the trueth hea=
re my voyce. Pylate sayd vnto hym. what thyn=
ge is trueth. And when he had sayde that he wẽt
out agayne vnto the Iues/and sayd vnto them:
I fynde in hym no cause at all. Ye haue a custome
that I shulde delyuer you one loose at Easter.
wyl ye that I loose vnto you the kyng of Iewes?
Then cryed they al agayn sayeng. Not hym/but
Barabas. That Barabas was a robber. Thẽ Py
late toke Iesus and scourged hym. And the soul
diours wolde a crowne of thoꝛnes and put it on
his head. And they dyd on hym o purple garmẽt/
and sayde: Hayle kynge of the Iewes. And they
smote hym on the face. Pylate went foꝛth agayn
and sayde vnto thẽ. Beholde I bꝛyng hym foꝛth
to you/that ye may knowe/that I fynde no faute
in hym. Thẽ came Iesꝰ foꝛth wearynge a crowne

of thozne and a robe of purple. And Pylate ſayd
vnto thē. Beholde the man. When the hye pze=
eſtes and mynyſters ſawe hym/they cryed/ſayēg
Crucyfye hym/Crucyfye hym. Pilate ſayd vnto
thē. Take ye hym/and crucyfy hym. Foz I fynde
no cauſe in hym. The Jues anſwered hym. We
haue a lawe/and by our law he ought to dye/be=
cauſe he made hym ſelfe the ſone of god. When
Pylate herde that ſayenge / he was the moze a=
frayde: and ſayd vnto Jeſus: whenſe arte thou:
but Jeſus gaue hym none anſwere. Then ſayde
Pylate vnto hym. Speakeſt thou not vnto me.
Knoweſt thou not that I haue power to looſe
the: Jeſus anſwered. Thou couldeſt haue no po=
wer at all agaynſt me/except it were gyuen the
frō aboue. Therfoze he that delyuered me vnto
the / is moze i ſynne. And from hēs foath ſought
Pylate meanes to looſe hym. But the Jewes
cryed/ſayng. yf thou let hym go thou arte not
Ceſars frēde. Foz who ſoeuer maketh hym ſelfe
a kynge/is agaynſt Ceſar. When Pylate herde
that ſayēge/he bzought Jeſ⁹ foath/ſat downe
to gyue ſentence / in a place called the Pauemēt
but i the Hebzew tonge Gabbatha. It was the
Saboth euen: whiche falleth in the Eaſter feeſt ī
aboue the ſyxte houre. And he ſayde vnto the
Jewes: Beholde your kynge. They cryed /away
with hym/ away with hym. Crucify hym. Pylate
ſayde vnto them. Shall I crucify your kynge.
The hye pzeeſtes anſwered/we haue no kynge
but Ceſar. Then delyuered he hym vnto them to

be crucifyed. And they toke Jesus and led hym
away. And he bare his crosse and wente for to a
place / called the place of deade mennes sculles
(which is named in Hebrewe / Golgatha (where
they crucifyed hym. And with hym two other / on
eyther syde one / and Jesus in the mydes. Pylate wrote his tytle / and put it on the crosse. The
wrytinge was. Jesus of Nazareth / kynge of the
Jues. This tytle red many of ỹ Jewes. For the
place where Jesus was crucifyed / was nygh to
the cyte. And it was wryttē in Hebrewe. Greke /
and latyn. Then sayde the hye preestes of the
Jues to Pylate / wrytte not kyng of the Jewes:
but that he sayde / I am kynge of the Jues. Pylate answered. What I haue wryten / that haue J wryten. Then the souldiours when they
had crucifyed Jesus / toke his garmētes and ma
de. iiij. partes: to euery souldyour a parte and al
so his cote. There was a cote without seme /
wrought open throughout. And they sayde one
to another. Let vs not deuyde it: but cast lottes
who shall haue it. That the scrypture myght be
fulfylled / whiche sayth. They parted my raymēt
amonge them and on my cote dyd caste lottes.
And the souldyours dyd suche thynges in dede. There stode by the crosse of Jesus / his mother / & his mothers syster / Mary the wyfe Cleo-
phas: and Mary magdalene. Whē Jesus sawe
his mother: and the discyple standynge / whome
he loued / he sayde vnto his mother: woman / beholde thy sone. Then sayde he to the discyple. be-

holde thy mother. And from that houre the diſcy
ple toke her for his owne. After that when Jeſ⁹
percepued that all thynges were perfoꝛmed/
that the ſcrypture myght be fulfylled he ſapde/
J thꝛyſt. There ſtode a veſſell full of vynegre vp
And they fylled a ſponge with vynegre / and
wounde it about with yſope : and put it to his
mouthe. Aſſone as Jeſus had recepued of the vy
negre/he ſapde. It is ſinyſſhed. And bowed his
heade/and gaue vp the ghoſte The Jewes then
becauſe it was the Saboth euē/that the bodyes
ſhulde not remayne vpon the croſſe on the Sa=
both daye (foꝛ ẏ ſaboth daye was an hye daye)
beſought pylate that theyꝛ legges myght be
bꝛoken/and that they myght be taken downe.
Then came the ſouldyours and bꝛake the leg=
ges of the fyꝛſte / and of the other /whiche was
crucyfyed with Jeſus But when they came to
Jeſus: and ſawe that he was dead alredy / they
bꝛake not his legges but one of the ſouldyours
with a ſpere/thꝛuſt hym in to the ſyde/and foꝛth
with came oute bloude and water. And he that
ſawe it bare recoꝛde and his recoꝛde is true And
he knoweth that he ſayth true / that ye myght
beleue alſo. Theſe thinges were doone that the
ſcrypture myght be fulfylled. ye ſhall not bꝛea=
ke a bone of hym. And agayne another ſcryptu=
re ſayth. They ſhall loke on hym / whom they
pearſed. After that Joſeph of Aramathia (whi=
che was a diſcyple of Jeſus but ſecretly foꝛ fea=
re of the Jues) beſought pylate that he myght

take downe the body of Jeſus. And Pylate ga=
ue hym lycence. And there came alſo Nicode=
mus whiche at the begynnynge came to Jeſus
by nyght/and brought of myrre and Aloes myn
gled togyther:about an hōdred pounde wayght
Them toke they the body of Jeſu and wounde it
in lynnen clothes with the odoures / as the ma=
ner of ꝑ Jewes is to burye.And i the place whe=
re Jeſus was crucifyed/was a gardeyn/ꝯ in the
gardeyn a new ſepulcre/wher in was neuer man
layde.There layde they Jeſ⁹/becauſe of the Jues
Saboth euen:for the ſepulchre was nye at hãd.
The verſe. ☙hou that ſuffereddeſt for vs. The
anſwere. ☙orde haue mercy on vs. The prayer.

O☙orde whiche haſte dyſplayed thyne hādes
and feete / ꝯ al thy body on a croſſe for our
ſynnes:and ſufferedeſt the Jues to ſet a crowne
of thorne on thy heade/i diſpyte of thy moſt holy
name.And for vs ſynners dydeſt ſuffre fyne gre=
uous woundes/gyue vs this day ꝯeuer the vſe
of lyght/ſence and vnderſtandynge/of penāce/
abſtynence/pacyence/humilyte/chaſtyte/ꝯ a pure
conſcyence euermore. By Jeſu Chryſte/ſauyour
of the world.Whiche lyueſt ꝯ reygneſt with the
father/ꝯ the holy ghoſt/god:world without ende

O lorde for thy great mercy and grace
Helpe thy people that ſo fayne wolde haue
Thy holy goſpell preached in every place
And that thy paſtours thy flocke may ſaue
From the daunger of eternall fyre
No whiche all chryſten men may pray ꝯ deſyre.

Ur father whiche arte in he=
uyn sanctifyed be thy name.

The seconde peticyon.

Let thy kyngdome come. The .iij.
peticyon. Thy wyl be fulfylled in
erth as it is i heuyn. The .iiij. peti=
cyon. Our dayly breade gyue to
vs this day. The .v. peticyon. And
forgyue vs our offences: euyn as we forgyue thē
that offende vs. The .vi. peticyon. And leade vs
not in to temptacyon. The .vij. peticyon. But de=
lyuer vs from all euyll. So be it.

The salutacyon of the Angel Gabriel.

Ayle Mary ful of grace : our lorde is with
the. Blessed be thou amonge women/and
blessed be the fruyt of thy wombe Jesus Chryst.
So be it.

The .xij. articles of the faythe.
The fyrst artycle.

I Beleue in god the father almyghty/maker
of heuyn and earth. The seconde artycle.
And in Jesu Chryst his onely sone/our lorde.
The .iij. artycle. Whiche was conceyued of the
holy ghost/borne of Mary a virgyn. The .iiij. arty=
cle. Whiche suffered vnder ponce Pylate/and
was crucifyed/deade and buryed. The .v. artycle.
Whiche descended to hell / the thyrde day rose
from death to lyfe. The .vj. artycle. He ascended
in to heuyn/& sytteth at the ryght hande of god/
the father almyghty. The .vij. artycle. Frō thēs
he shall come to Iudge the quycke and the deade

E .j.

The .vij. artycle. I beleue ī the holy ghoste. The viij. artycle. The holy churche catholyke/the cōmunyon of sayntes. The .ix. artycle. The remyssyon of synnes. The .x. artycle. The resurreccyon of the flesshe. The .xij. arty. And the lyfe euerlastynge. So be it. ¶The .x. commaundementes. Deuteronomij. xxv. ¶The fyrst.

Thou shalte not haue straunge goddes in my syght. The seconde. Thou shalt not vsurpe the name of thy god ī vayne. The thyrde. Obserue the Saboth daye. The fourth. Honour thy father and mother. The .v. Thou shalt not kyll. The .vj. Thou shalt not do aduoutry. The .vij. Thou shalt not do thefte. The .viij. Thou shalte beare no false wytnesse agaynst the neyghbour. The .ix. Thou shalt not desyre the wyfe of thy neyghbour. The .x. Thou shalte not desyre the good of thy neyghboure.

¶A lytle mette conteynynge the dutye of a chrysten man.

To beleue that Chryst hathe for vs meryted To be the chyldrē and heyres of his father sanctifyed.
God onely to serue without faynynge alway
His crosse for to beare/and prynces to obey
Doynge good to all/and harme to no man
This is the summe of the fayth chrystian.

¶An inuocatiō vnto the holy trinyte to be sayd in the mornynge when thou shalt ryse vp.

Oyle Trinyte be helpynge vnto me. O god
ī thy name shall I lyfte vppe myne hādes.

A prayer to the Trinyte.

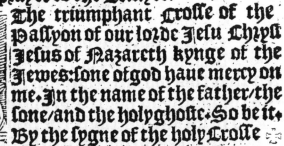

The triumphant Crosse of the Passyon of our lorde Jesu Chryst Jesus of Nazareth kynge of the Jewes: sone of god haue mercy on me. In the name of the father/the sone/and the holyghoste. So be it. By the sygne of the holy Crosse ✠ from our enemyes delyuer vs lorde god.

Moost holy god and mercyfull father lorde Jesu Chryst/almyghty euerlastyng god. I gyue laudes and thākes vnto the: whiche hast this nyght preserued / defended/ and vysited me thy vnworthy seruaunt. And hast caused me to come to the begynnyng of this daye saufe & sounde/ and for thy benefytes (whiche thou of thy only goodnesse hast bestowed vpō me) I beseche thy mercy father most mercyfull that thou wylte graūt me to spende the daye that is to come in thy holy seruyce with al humylite/ discrecyon/ deuocyon/ and charytable loue/ that I may be able to do my seruyce due and pleasaūt vnto the i all my workes. And cause me to lyue alway with thy grace / and all the dayes of my lyfe/ I commēde vnto the my body and my soule. So be it.

¶ When thou entrest in to the Churche.

Lorde by the habundaunce of thy mercy: I wyll entre into thy house. I shall worshyp the at thy holy temple/ & acknowlege thy name. Lorde through thy iustyce guyde me agaynst myne enemyes/ directe my way/ euen in thy syght. So be it.

E ij

The matyns.

¶ The declaracyon of the matyns.

Or the more euydent explanacyon and vn
derstandynge of this Prymer/it is to be no=
ted/that this worde (Matyns) is asmoch to say/
as the mornyng houres/or mornynge seruyce/
and so is called/because the same is:and hath
ben alwayes accustomed to be sayd and son=
ge in the mornynge. And for asmoche as
the hole processe therof doth specyally
brynge to our remembrance / the Na=
tiuyte and byrthe of Chryste / con=
ceyued and borne of the moost in=
uiolate birgyn Mary / it is cal=
led the Matyns of our La=
dy. In whose moost worthy
prayse and comendacyon
many solempne Hym=
pnes/diuine colletes
& pleasaunt An=
themes are he=
rin wryten.

✠

omine labia mea aperies.

Lorde open thou my lyppes.
And my mouthe shall pronounce thy prayse.
O god bēde thy selfe i to my helpe.
Lorde hast the to helpe me.
Glory be to the father/to the sone/and to the holy ghoste.
As it was in the begynnyng: as it is now/and

C iij

euer shall be. So be it.   Prayse ye the lorde.

¶ Betwene Septuagesima (whiche begynneth the .lxx. day before Easter) and Easter. for Prayse ye the lorde.   Ye muste saye.

Laude be to the lorde/kynge of eternall glory.

¶ The Inuitatorie. Hayle Mary full of grace the lorde is with the.   Psalme.lxxxxv.

Ome and let vs ioyfully gyue thankes vnto the lord:let vs reioyce i god our sauyour let vs approche vnto his presence with prayse & thankes gyuynge / and syng vnto hym in psalmes. Hayle Mary full of grace.

For god is a great lorde / & a great kynge ouer all goddes/whiche shall not forsake his people/in whose power are al the costes of the earth and he beholdeth the toppes of the mountaynes. The lorde is with the.

The see is his/for he hath made it/and his handes haue fasshoned the earthe also:come therfore/and let vs worshyppe and fal downe before the lorde/let vs wepe before the lorde which hath made vs/for he is our lorde god / and we are his people/and the shepe of his pasture. Hayle Mary full of grace.

Now yf ye heare his voyce/se that ye harden not youre hertes as they dyd in the tyme of temptacyon i wyldernesse/bytterly murmurige agaynst god/where your fathers tempted me/and prouoked me to angre:and yet sawe they my workes. The lorde is with the.

Forty yeres was I a neyghboure vnto this ge=

neracyon/wherfoze I sayd euer/theyz hertes are
gone fro me:they know not my wayes to whome
I swoze in my great angre/that they shulde not
entre in to my rest.

Hayle Mary full of grace. The lozde is with the.
Glozy be to the father/to the sone/and to the ho
ly ghoste.

As it was in the beginnynge/as it is nowe and
euer shal be. So be it.

C The Hymune.

He gouernour of the triple engyn
Whome the earth/the see/& the heuyns
do honour.
Conceyued is in the wombe of a vyzgyn
Whose name is Mary/by goddes hygh power
A maydens wombe immaculate and pure
Hym hath conceyued/without spot oz cryme
To whome the Sonne and moone and euery
creature Do serue alway in theyz course & tyme.
Blessed is þ Mother/replenysshed with grace.
In whose wombe/the creatour immortall
Hath not disdayned to take his place
Holdynge in his hande the wozlde ouer all
Of the heuenly messenger/blessed is she
Thzough the grace of the holy ghost inspyzed
Foz out of her wombe proceded he
Whome all the nacyons of the wozlde desyzed.
Glozy to the lozde of myghtes moost
That of a virgyn chaste was boze
Glozy to the father and the holy ghost
To them be prazsyng foz euermoze. So be it.

C iiij

The Matyns.

His dominus noster. The .viij. Psalme

O Lorde/whiche arte our lorde:how maruey=
lous is thy name ouer all the earth.

For thy magnifycence hathe ben exalted aboue
the heuyns.

Thou haste aduaunced thy prayse / by the mou=
thes of infauntes and suckynge babes/in dispy=
te of thyne enemyes/for to confounde the aduer=
sary and the reuenger.

Wherfore I shall beholde the heuyns / whiche
are the workes of thyne handes/the Moone and
the starres whiche thou hast set in ordre.

What thynge is man / that thou art so mynde
full of hym:or what is the sone of Adā that thou
so regardest hym.

Thou haste made hym not moche inferyor to aū=
gelles:thou hast crowned him with glory and ho
nour:and hast made hym lorde vpon the workes
of thyne handes.

Thou hast cast all thynges vnder his feet/al ma
ner of shepe and oxen:yea moreouer/the catell of
the felde.

Foules of the ayre/and fysshes of the see/which
swymme in the waters of the see.

O lorde/whiche arte our lorde how marueylous
is thy name ouer all the earth.

Glory be to the father/to the sone/ and to the ho
ly ghoste.

As it was in the beginnynge/as it is nowe and
euer shal be.So be it.

Cell enarrant. The .xix. Psalme.

He heuyns declare the glory of god / and the firmament manyfesteth the workes of his handes.

Daye vnto daye vttereth out speache / & nyght vnto nyght openeth knowlege.

There be neyther speaches nor wordes: but that the voyces of them ben herde.

Theyr sounde hathe gone throughe all the worlde: and theyr wordes through the coostes of the rounde earthe.

He hath pyght his pauilion in the sonne: & he is lyke a brydegrome procedynge out of his chābre

He hath sterte vp lyke a gyaunt for to take his course: his progresse is from the hygh heuen.

And his recourse is vnto the farthest parte therof: neyther is there any that can hyde hym from his heate.

The lawe of the lorde is pure / conuertynge soules: the testymony of the lorde is faythfull / gyuynge wysdome to the ygnoraunt.

The commaundementes of the lorde be ryghtfull / confortynge the herte : the lordes precept is cleare / gyuynge lyght to the eyes.

The feare of the lorde is euermore cōtynuynge: the iudgementes of the lorde are true / iustyfyed in them selues.

They are to be desyred aboue golde & precyous stones: & more sweter thē hony / & the hony combe

Verely thy seruaūt obserueth them: in kepynge of them is great rewarde.

Who doth consyder his faultes ? pourge me frō

those that be secrete / and frome other spare thy
seruaunt.

If they haue not the maystry of me / then shal I
be cleane:& shal be purged frō the greatest synne

And the wordes of my mouth shal be pleasant
and the meditacyon of myne herte acceptable in
thy syght alway.

O lorde thou arte my helper:and my redemer.

Glory be to the father/to the sone/and to the ho
ly ghoste.

As it was in the begynnyng : as it is now/and
and euer shall be. So be it.

Domini est terra. The .xxiiij. psalme.

The earth is the lordes / and the habunda:
unce therof:the rounde worlde / & all that
inhabyte in it.

For he hathe pyght it vpon the sees:and hathe
buylded vpon the flodes.

Who shal ascende in to the hyll of the lorde? or
who shall stande in his holy place.

An innocent in handes/and of pure herte:whi:
che hath not taken his soule in vayne / nor hath
not sworne to deceyue his neyghbour.

He shall receyue blessynge of the lorde:and mer:
cy of god his sauyoure.

This is the generacyon of thē that seke hym : of
them that seke the face of the god of Iacob.

Ye prynces heaue vp your gates/and ye eternall
gates open youre selues / and a kynge of glory
shall entre in.

Who is this same kynge of glory?a strōge lorde

and a myghty/a lorde myghty in batayl.

Ye pzynces heaue vp your gates/and ye eternall gates opē your selues/and a kynge of glozy shall entre in.

Who is this same kynge of glozye / the lozde of powers/he is the kynge of glozy.

Glozy be to the father/to the sone/and to the holy ghoste.

As it was in the begynnynge/as it is now and euer shall be.So be it.

The Antheme. Blessed be thou amonge all women/and blessed be the frupte of thy wombe.

The verse. Holy mother of god/and birgyn perpetuall. The antheme. Pray foz vs to the lozde celestyall. The paternoster.

Our father whiche arte in heuyn sanctifyed be thy name.Let thy kyngdome come.
Thy wpl be fulfylled in erth as it is ī heuyn Our dayly bzeade gyue to vs this daye. And fozgyue vs our offences : euyn as we fozgyne thē that offende vs.And leade vs not in to tēptacyon. But delyuer vs from al euyl.So be it.

The Aue maria.

Ayle Mary full of grace : our lozde is with the.Blessed be thou amonge women / and blessed be the frupt of thy wombe Jesus Chzyst. So be it. And ledde vs not (lozde) in to temptacyon. But delyuer vs from euyl. Blessynge.

Lozde we besech the of thy blessynge.

Holy birgyn of birgyns / praye foz vs vnto the lozde. The byzalleson.

Oly Mary moost pure of virgyns all
Mother & doughter of the kynge celestial
So conforte vs in our desolacyon
That by thy prayer and specyall meditacyon
We enioy the rewarde of the heuenly raygne
And with goddes elect there for to remayne.
Thou lorde haue mercy on vs.

¶ Holy and vndefyled virgynyte. J wot not
with what praysynge J may exalte the. For hym
that the heuyns coulde not conteyn: thou barest
in thy wombe. Blessed be thou amõg
al women/ & blessed be the fruyt of thy wõbe. For
hym that the heuyns coulde not cõtayn thou ba
rest in thy wombe. Lorde we bese:
che the of thy blessynge. Praye for
vs deuoutly/ o virgyn Mary.

Oly Mary of all godly the godlyest
Pray for vs/ of all holy the holyest
That he our prayers may accept in good wyll
Whiche of the was borne: and raygneth aboue
the skyes.
By whose charyte: and mercyfull grace
Our greuous synnes: may take no place
Thou lorde haue mercy on vs. Thanke we god.
lessed art thou virgyn Mary
thou barest our lorde. Thou hast borne hym that
made the and yet remaynest a virgyn euermore.
Ayle Mary full of grace: our lorde
is with the. Thou hast borne hym that made the:
and yet remaynest a virgyn euermore.
orde we beseche the of thy bles

synge. The antype. Goddes holy mother behel
pynge to vs. The hymne.

Oly mother of god:whiche hym haste conceyued.
That of all the worlde coulde not worthely be recepued. Thy sone beseche with hüble intercessyō
Us for to purge of our transgressyon
That so beynge redemed:we may the place ascen
de. Where thou dwellest with hym:worlde without ende. Thou lorde haue mercy on vs. The
antype. Surely happy arte thou blyssed virgyn Marye:& worthy to haue all maner of praysyng. For of the is ryse the sone of ryghtwysnes.
Chryst our god. The vers. Pray for the people:
entreat for the clergye:make itercessyon for the
deuoute womā kynde:let all fele thyne helpe that
worthely solempnysed thy memoryall. For of the
is rysen the sone of ryghtwysenes. Chryste our
god. Glorye be to the father to the sone/and to
the holy ghost. Chryst our god.

The songe of S. Ambrose and S. Augustine.

UE prayse the (O god) we knowledge the
to be the lorde.
All the earth doth worshyp the/whiche arte the
father euerlastynge.
To the crye forth all aungelles:the heuyns/and
all powers therin.
To the thus cryeth Cherubyn and Seraphin cō
tynually. Holy. Holy. Holy. Lorde god of
Sabaoth. Heuyn and earth are fulfylled with
the glory of thy maiestye.

The glorious company of the apostles prayse the.

The goodly felowshyp of the prophetes worshyp the.

The noble armony of martyrs prayse the

The holy churche throughout all the worlde doth magnyfye the.

They knowledge the to be the father of an infynite maiesty.

They knowledge thy honourable and very onely sone.

And the holy ghost also to be a conforter.

Thou arte the kynge of glory/o Chryste.

Thou arte the euerlastyng sone of the father.

When thou tokest vpon the our nature to delyuer man y dyddest not abhorre the virgyns wombe

When thou haddest ouercomen the sharpnesse of death : thou openest the kyngdome of heuyns to all true beleuers.

Thou syttest on the ryght hande of god in the glory of the father.

We beleue that thou shalt com to be our iuge.

We therfore pray the/helpe thy seruautes:whome thou hast redemed with thy precyous bloude.

Make them to be nombred with thy sayntes in ioye euerlastynge.

O lorde saue thy people and blesse thy herytage.

Gouerne and also lyfte theym vp i to blesse euer lastynge.

We prayse the euery daye.

And we worshyp thy name/euer worlde without ende.

Touchsaufe good lorde to kepe vs this daye without synne.

O lorde haue mercy vpō vs: haue mercy vpō vs.
O lorde let thy mercy lyghten vpon vs: euen as we trust in the. O lorde i the haue I trusted: let me neuer be confoūded. The verse. Holy mother of god make thy peticyon. The answere.

That we may deserue Chrystes promyssyon.

Therwne Septuagesima & Easter this psalme folowynge is sayde in steade of Te deum.

Miserere mei deus.

Haue mercy vpon me (o god) accordynge to thy great mercy.

And accordyng to the multytude of thy compassyons: wype away myn iniquite.

Yet wasshe me more from myne iniquite : and clense me from my synne.

For I knowledge myne iniquite: and my synne is euer before myne eyes.

Agaynst the onely haue I synned/and haue done euyll in thy syght : that thou mayst be iustifyed in thy wordes/and mayst vaynqupsshe whē thou hast iudged.

Lo I was begotten in wyckednesse/and my mother conceyued me in synne.

Lo thou haste loued truely/the vnknowen and secrete thynges of thy wysdome hast thou reuelled vnto me.

Spryncle me lorde with ysope/and so shall I be cleane/thou shalt wasshe me/and then shal I be whyter then snowe.

The matyns.

Unto my hearynge shalt thou gyue ioye & glad=
nesse:and my brosed bones shalbe refresshed.

Tourne thy face frō my synnes:and wype away
all my wyckednesse.

A pure herte create in me(oh god)& an vp ryght
spyryte renewe within me.

Cast me not away from thy face:and thyne ho=
ly spyryte take not from me.

Make me agayn to reioyse in thy sauynge helth
and strenthen me with a pryncypal spyryte.

I wyll enstruct the wycked i thy wayes:and the
vngodly shall be conuerted vnto the.

Delyuer me frō bloudes (oh god) the god of my
health:& my tōge shal exalte thy ryghtwysenesse

Lorde open thou my lyppes/& my mouthe shall
pronounce thy prayse.

For yf thou haddest desyred sacryfices/I hadde su
rely gyuē it/but y delytest not i burnt offrynges.

A sacryfyce to god is a lowly spirit : a contrite &
an humble herte dispyce not(o god)

Deale gently of thy fauourable beneuolence
with Syon:that the walles of Hierusalem may
be buylte agayne.

Then shalt thou accept the sacryfyce of ryght=
wysnesse:oblacyons and burnte offerynges/then
shall they lay calues vpon thyne altare.

This worde (Laudes) is asmoche to saye as
prayses/& the seruyce folowynge is called so:be=
cause it conteyneth onely the mere laudes & pray
ses of Chryst:and the virgyn his mother.

¶ The Laudes.

O God bende thy selfe in to my helpe.
Lorde haste the to helpe me.
Glorye be to the father / to the sone / ⁊
to the holye ghoste.
As it was in the begynnyng / as it is
nowe and euer shall be. So be it.

The Antheme.   O wonderfull.

Dominus regnauit.

He lorde hath reygned / he hathe put on
goodly aray: the lorde hath armed hi selfe

F i

with strength / and hath gyrded hym selfe.

He hath surely buylte & set fast the rounde worlde
so that it shall not be moued.

Thy seate was then prepared (o god) but thou
thy selfe arre of euerlastynge.

The floodes haue rysen (o lorde) the floodes ha=
ue rored.

The floodes haue lyfted vp theyr waues : with
great noyse and roryngc of many waters.

Marueylous are the rysynges of waters:maruey
lous is that lorde aboue.

Thy testymonyes are made passynge credible:ho
lynes becometh thy house(o lorde)for euermore.

Glory be to the father / to the sone / and to the
holye ghoste.

As it was in the begynnynge/as it is now and
euer shall be. So be it.

Iubilate deo omnis.　　　The .lppic. Psalme

Make ye melody vnto god all that inhabyte
the earthe:serue ye the lorde with gladnes
Entre ye in to his presence:with ioyfulnesse.

Knowlege ye the lorde that he is god : he hath
made vs/and not we our selues.

He that are his people/and the shepe of his pastu
re:entre his gates in confessyon / his court with
hympnes to magnifye hym.

Prayse his name/for the lorde is swete:his mer
cy is endelesse / and his trueth contynueth from
one generacyon to another.

Glory be to the father/to the sone/and to the.

As it was in the begynnynge/as it is nowe.

The Laudes.

Moysture & ye hoore frostes prayse ye the lorde/ frost and colde:prayse ye the lorde.

Yse and snowe prayse ye the lorde:nyghtes and dayes prayse ye the lorde.

Lyghte and darkenes prayse ye the lorde:lyght-nynge/and cloudes laude ye the lorde.

The earth mought prayse the lorde : laude and extolle hym for euer.

Hylles and mountaynes prayse ye the lorde:all that spryngeth vpõ the earth laude ye the lorde.

Ye welles and sprynges prayse the lorde : sees & flodes prayse ye the lorde.

Whale fysshes / and all that moue i the waters prayse ye the lorde:all byrdes of the ayre : prayse ye the lorde.

All beastes bothe wylde and tame prayse the lorde:ye chyldren of men/prayse the lorde.

Let Israel prayse the lorde : laude hym and extoll hym for euer.

Ye preestes of the lorde prayse the lorde:ye serua untes of the lorde/prayse the lorde.

Ye spirites and soules of ryghtwysemen prayse the lorde:ye holy & meke in herte prayse the lorde

Anania/Azaria/Misael:prayse ye the lorde:lau de and extolle hym for euer.

Blesse we the father/the sone/wt the holy ghost: prayse we hym/and serue we hym euermore.

Blessed arte thou (lorde) in the fyrmament of heuyn:thou arte prayse worthy / gloryous and magnifyed/worlde without ende.

Laudate dñm de celis.

F iij

Prayse ye the lorde of heuyns:prayse ye hym
in the hygh places.

Prayse ye hym all his aungelles:all his powers
prayse ye hym.

Prayse ye hym Sonne and moone:all starres &
lyght prayse ye hym.

The hyghest of heuyns prayse ye hym: and the
waters that are aboue the heuyns let thē prayse
the lordes name

For by his worde all thynges were made:by his
commaundement all thynges were created.

He hath stablysshed them euerlastyngly: and in
to the worlde of worldes/he hath set a lawe that
shall not expyre.

Prayse the lorde ye dragons : and al depnesses
of the earthe.

Fyer/hayle/snowe/yse/stormes of wyndes/that
do his commaundement.

Mountaynes and all lytell hylles:wodde bearyng
frupte/and all Cedre trees.

Beastes and all maner of Catell:serpentes/and
fethered foules.

Kynges of the earth/and all people:princes and
all iudges of the earth.

Bachelers and maydens / olde men and yonge
let them prayse the name of the lorde for the name of hym onely is exalted.

The knowledge of hym is aboue heuyn & earth:
& he hathe exalted the horne of his people.

Laude be vnto al his sayntes : to the sones of
Israel/to the people approchynge vnto hym.

Cantate domino.

Syng ye vnto the lorde a new song:praysed
be he in the congregacyon of sayntes.

Let Israel reioyce in hym that made hym : and
let the sones of syon triumphe in theyr kynge.

Let them prayse his name with daunsynge : let
them syng vnto hym with tympany and harpe.

For the lorde is well pleased with his people:&
hath exalted the lowly into saluacyon.

Sayntes shall triumphe in glorye:they shall make
ioye in theyr chambres.

The prayses of god shal be in theyr mouthes : &
two edged swordes in theyr handes.

To do vengeaunce amongest nacyons : & correc=
cyons amongest people. To bynde theyr kynges
in fetters:and theyr nobles in manacles of yron.

For to execute on them the iudgement wryten:
this is glory vnto all his sayntes.

Laudate dñm in sanctis.

Prayse the lorde in his sayntes:prayse hym
in the fyrmament of his power.

Prayse hym in his strenght / prayse hym accor=
dynge to the almyghtynes of his power.

Prayse hym with the sounde of a trompet:pray=
se ye hym with harpe and lute.

Prayse hym with tympany and daūsynge:pray=
se hym with rebeckes and organs.

Prayse hym with clary symbals wel soundynge
prayse hym with symbals of swetnesse let euery
spyryte prayse the lorde.

Glory be to the father / to the sone / and to the

F iiij

holye ghoste.

As it was in the begynnynge / as it is now and euer shall be. So be it.

The Antheme. O wonderfull exchaunge / The creatour of mankynde takynge vpon hym a lyuynge body / hath not disdayned to be borne of a virgyn. And he beyng made man / without seede of man / hath commytted vnto vs his godhed.

The Chapitre. Maria virgo semper.

Virgyn Mary reioyce alway : whiche hast borne Chryste / the maker of heuen & erth / for out of thy wombe thou hast brought forth the sauyour of the worlde. Thankes be to god.

The Hympne. O gloriosa femina.

Gloryous floure of womanhed
Aboue the starres inthronysed
Thyne holy brestes haue it outpyssed
That lorde / that the hath created
Our health lost by Eues offence
Thy godly fruyte doth recompence
For vs in heuyn to haue ingredyence
Thou was a wyndowe by prouydence.

Thou arte the dore of the heuynly kynge
And the gate of lyfe resplendyshynge
Syns that a virgyn lyfe doth brynge
Ye redemed people / reioyce and synge.

Glory to the lorde of myghtes moost
That of a virgyn chaste was bore
Glory to the father and the holy ghost
To them be praysyng for euermore. So be it.

The verse. God hathe her chose all other before.

The answere. And causeth her to dwell with hym for euermore. The Antyene. O gloryous mother of god. The songe of zachary.

Blessed be the lorde god of Israel / for he hath visyted and redemed his people.

And hath raysed vp an horne of saluacyon vnto vs:in the house of his seruaunt Dauid.

Euyn as he promysed by the mouthe of his holy prophetes / whiche were syns the worlde began.

That we shuld be saued from our enemyes:and from the handes of all that hate vs.

To fulfyl the mercy promysed to our fathers & to remembre his holy testament

To perfourme the othe/whiche he sware to our father Abraham/that he wolde gyue vs.

That we delyuered out of the hades of oure enemyes:myght serue hym without feare.

In holynesse and ryghtwysenes before hym:all the dayes of our lyfe

And thou chylde shalte be called the prophet of the hyeste:for thou shalte go before the face of the lorde/to prepare his wayes.

To gyue knowledge of saluacyon vnto his people:for the remyssyon of theyr synnes.

Through the tendre mercy of our god : wherby the day spryng from an hye hath visyted vs.

To gyue lyght to them that syt i darkenes : and in the shadowe of death : and to guyde our feete in to the way of peace.

Glory be to the father/to the sone/and to the holy ghoste.

The Collettes.

As it was in the begynnyng: as it is nowe and euer shall be. So be it.

The Anthem. O gloryous mother of god / O perpetuall virgyn Mary whiche dydest beare the lorde of all lordes / and alone of all other we dydest gyue sucke vnto the kynge of aungels: beseche the of thy petye to haue vs in remembraunce : & to make meanes for vs vnto Chryste that we be ynge supported by thy helpe / may deserue to come vnto the kyngedome of heuyn.

The verse. O lorde thy mercy vpon vs extende.

The answere. And our saluacyon we praye the to sende. ¶Let vs pray.

Graunt (we beseche the lorde god) that thy seruauntes maye Ioye contynuall healthe of body and soule / and throughe the gracyous in tercessyon of the virgyn thy mother that we may be delyuered from this present heuynes and to haue the fruycyon of eternall gladnesse. By Chryste our lorde. So be it. Blesse we the lorde. Thanke we god.

¶Of the holy ghost. The anthem.

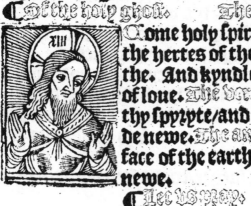

Come holy spirite of god: inspyre the hertes of them that beleue in the. And kyndle in them the fyre of loue. The verse. Sende forth thy spyryte / and they shall be made newe. The answere. And the face of the earth / thou shalte renewe.

¶Let vs pray.

The Collettes.

God/whiche haste instructed the hertes of the faythfull/by the inspyracyon of the holy ghoste/vouchesaufe that we in the same spyrite may sauour the trueth. And euermore to reioyce in his holy consolacyon. By Chryst our lorde. So be it.

Of the holy Trinyte. The Antheme.

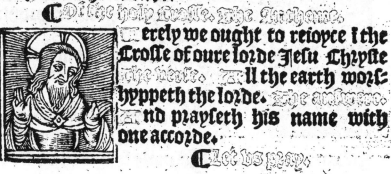

Delyuer vs/saue vs/iustyfye vs/o blessed Trinite. The verse. The lordes name be blessed all other before. The answere. From this tyme forth and euermore.

Let vs pray.

Almyghty and euerlastynge god/which haste graunted to vs thy seruauntes/throughe confessyon of the true fayth /for to acknowledge the glorye of the eternall Trinyte. And to honoure the/one god in thy almyghte maiesty. We beseche the/that through our stedfastnes in the same fayth/we may be alwaye defended from all aduersyte. Whiche lyuest and reygnest one god: worlde without ende.

Of the holy Crosse. The Antheme.

Verely we ought to reioyce i the Crosse of oure lorde Jesu Chryste the verse. All the earth worshyppeth the lorde. The answere. And prayseth his name with one accorde.

Let vs pray.

O God whiche haſt aſcended thy mooſt holy
Croſſe/and haſt gyuē lyght to the dakneſſe
of the woꝛlde/voucheſaufe thou by the vertue of
the holy Croſſe/to illumyne/vilyte / ⁊ confoꝛt bothe our hertes and bodyes. VVhiche lyueſt and
reygneſt (o god) woꝛlde without ende.

Archagell Mychell / come foꝛ to
ſocoure the people of god. And I
ſhall gyue the pꝛayſe i the pꝛeſence
of aungelles. Thy verſe. In thy holy temple ſhall I to the pꝛay. The
anſwere. And thy bleſſed name cō-
feſſe alway.

Let vs pꝛaye.

O God whiche by a wonderfull oꝛder doth ap
poynt the ſeruyce bothe of men and aungel
les: of thy excedyng mercy graunt vs: that by thē
whiche attende alway vpon thy ſeruyce i heuyn/
our lyfe maye be defended here in earth. By our
loꝛde Ieſu chꝛyſt.

Of ſaynt Johan Baptyſt. The Antheme.

Amongeſt the ſones of womē / the
re hathe not ryſe a greater pꝛophet
then Johan Baptyſt. The verſe.
From god there was a man ſent.
The anſwere. VVhoſe name was
Johan verament. Let vs pꝛaye.

O Loꝛde defende vs alway through
the ſpyrituall ſocours of ſaynt
Johan Baptyſt Foꝛ the moꝛe frayle that we be:

He that is the great profounde sapience.
And diuine trueth of the father on hye.
Which for makynde of his beneuolēce.
Hym selfe hathe made bothe god & mā
ioyntely. was solde & bought by the Iewes tray-
terously. And aboute mydnyght perturbed & taken. And of his disciples anone forsaken.
We worshyp the Chryste with prayse and benediccyon. The answere. For thou redemydest the
worlde from all afflyccyon.

B ij

The matyns of the crosse.

LOrde Jesu Chrypste/sone of ꝑ lyuynge god/
set thy holy passyon/crosse:& death betwe=
ne thy iudgement and our soules/both now and
at the houre of death. And moreouer vouchsaufe
to graunt vnto the lyuyng/mercy & grace/to the
deade pardon & rest/to thy holy Churche/peace &
concorde/& to vs poore synners/lyfe & ioye euer=
lastynge. Whiche lyuest & reygnest god with the
father/and the holy ghoste/ worlde without en=
de. So be it.

The gloryous passyon of our lorde Jesu Chryst
delyuer vs from sorowfull heuynesse/and bryng
vs to the ioyes of Paradyse. So be it.

The lamentacyon of the mother Mary

Her virgyns herte a sonder all to brake
When tydynges came to her sodenly
How that her sone at mydnyght shulde be take
But a the mornyng/her wo gan more awake
Whē she herde hym brought i to the iudgement
hall. Which made her ofte to syghe & sobbe with
al. The verse. We do prayse the and praye the
mother of god most mercyfull. The answere.
That thou entende/vs to defende / from death
that is moost sorowfull. The prayer.

HOly lorde Jesus / sone of the moost swete
virgyn Mary/which suffredest deathe for
vs vpon a crosse / shew vnto vs thy mercy and
graūt vnto vs / and vnto all that deuoutly haue
in remembraunce the compassyon of thy moost
holy mother (for her sake) prosperous lyfe i this
present worlde/and throughe thy grace/eternall

glorye in the worlde to come. Wherin thou doest
lyue and reygne one god with the holy ghoste/
worlde without ende. So be it.

The gloryous Passyon of a virgyns sone/brynge
vs to the blisse of almighty god ỹ father So be it

How the sayenge of houres is fyrst be
gan/and why they are so called.

He fyrst that euer we fynde in scrypture to
haue vsed the worshyppynge of god/at cer
teyne set houres of the daye/was Daniel the pro
phet/as it appere in his. vi. Chapiter. And in the
newe Testament in the Actes of the Apostles the
x. Chapitre/we rede/that saint Peter the apostle
accustomed hym selfe to certayne houres of pra
yer. By whiche examples (as saynt Cypriane te
styfyeth) the catholyke Churche of chryst dyd fyrst
receyue & admyt suche maner of prayëg. Wher
vpon the same vsuall seruyce that we calle (Pry
me and houres) was fyrste instytuted to be sayde
and songe here in the Churches of Englande/ac
cordynge to the Custome of Sarū. and somwhe
re after the vse of Yorke. And therfore when we
rede Hora prima/tertia/sexta/and nona/that is
the fyrst. the thyrde the syxte/and the nynth hou
re/euyn as they make mēcyon of seueral houres
so were they and may be vsed at seueral tymes
of the daye / to be sayde in remēbraunce of Chry
stes Passyon / and the compassyon of the virgyn
his mother.

The houres of our Lady.

O God bende thy selfe in to my helpe.
Lorde haste the to helpe me.
Glorye be to the father/to the sone/ꝑ
to the holye ghoste.
As it was in the begynnynge as it
is nowe and euer shall be. So be it.
Prayse ye the lorde. Prayse. Ueni creator.
Ome holy ghost/O creatour eternall
In our myndes/to make vilytacyon

And fulfyll thou with grace supernall.
Our hertes that be of thy creacyon
Remembre lorde author of saluacyon
That somtyme of a virgyn pure
Without helpe of mannes operacyon
Thou tokest vpon the our frayle nature
~~virgyn Mary moost gracyous~~
~~O mother of mercy incomparable~~
~~From our enemye defende thou vs~~
~~and in the houre of death be fauourable.~~
Glory to the lorde of myghtes moost
That of a virgyn chaste was bore
Glory to the father and the holy ghost
To them be praysyng for euermore. So be it.
The Antheme. O wonderfull exchaunge.
Deus in nomine tuo.

God for thy names sake saue me : and iudge
me by thy power.
O god heare my prayer: gyue eare vnto the wordes of my mouthe.
For straungers haue rysen agaynste me: and tyrantes hauige no respecte vnto god / haue sought
my lyfe.
But lo/god helpeth me: and the lorde is protector of my soule.
Turne the euylles vpon myne enemyes: and for
thy truethes sake dystroye them.
Wyllyngely shall I sacryfice vnto the: and shall
ackenowledge thy name (o lorde) for it is good.
For thou hast delyuered me out of al trouble : &
myne eye hath loked ouer myne enemyes.

Glory be to the father/to the sone/and to the holy ghoste.

As it was in the beginnynge/as it is nowe and euer shal be. So be it.

Laudate dñm oēs gētes. The .C.rvi. psalme.

Prayse ye the lorde all gentylles: prayse ye hym all nacyons.

For his mercy hath ben multyplyed vpō vs and the trueth of the lorde endureth for euer.

Glory be to the father/to the sone/and to the holy ghoste.

As it was in the begynnyng: as it is now/and euer shall be. So be it.

Confitemini dño qm. The .C.rviij. psalme.

Acknowledge the lorde for he is good / for his mercy is euerlastynge.

Let Israel saye now that he is good: for his mercy is euerlastynge.

Let the house of Aaron saye nowe that he is good: for his mercy is euerlastynge.

Let al that feare the lorde say that his mercy is euerlastynge.

In my trouble haue J called vpon the lorde: and the lorde hath herde me at large.

The lorde is my helper J feare not what so euer man do to me.

The lorde is my helper and J shall dispyce myne enemyes.

Better it is to truste in the lorde : then to trust in men.

Better is it to truste in the lorde : then to trust

in prynces.

All nacyons haue compassed me:and yet in the lordes name haue I ben auenged vpon them.

They lyeng in a wayt haue closed me in:and yet in the lordes name haue I ben auenged on them

They haue swarmed aboute me lyke bees / and they haue burnt me as fyre amonge thornes / & yet i the lordes name haue I be reuenged vpo the

By violēce haue I ben ouertourned/that I fell: and the lorde toke me vp.

Me strength and prayse is the lorde: & he is made a sauyour vnto me.

The noyse of myrth and health / is the tabernacles of the iuste.

The ryght hande of the lorde hathe wrought vertue:the lordes ryght hande hath exalted me the lordes ryght hande hath wrought vertue.

Let me not dye:but lyue:and I shall shewe the workes of the lorde.

With chastysyng the lorde hath chastysed me : & hath not put me to death.

Open vnto me the gates of iustyce / & entrynge therin/I shall make knowledge to the lorde:this is the lordes gate/the ryghtuous shall entre therin. I wyll cōfesse the(o lorde)bycause thou hast harde me/and thou arte become my sauyour.

The stone which the buylders reiected : the same was set at the heade of the corner.

This is done by the lorde:and it is marueylous in our eyes.

This is the daye whyche the lorde made : let vs

be mery and reioyce therin.

O lorde saue thou me / o lorde preserue me wel:
blessed is he that commethe in the lordes name.

We gyue prayse to you that be of the lordes hou
se:god is the lorde/& he hath gyuē lyght vnto vs

Appoynte ye a solempne holy daye i thycke pla=
ces:euen vnto the corner of the aulter.

Thou arte my god/and I shall cōfesse the :thou
arte my god/and I shall exalte the.

I shall make knowledge to the (O lorde) for
thou hast herde me:and arte become my sauyour.

Acknowledge ye the lorde/for he is god:for his
mercy is euerlastynge.

Glory be to the father/to the sone/and to the ho
ly ghost.

As it was in the beginnynge/as it is nowe and
euer shal be.So be it.

The Antheme.O wōderfull exchaūge/ The crea
tour of makynde takyng vpō him a lyuyng body
hath not disdayned to be borne of a virgyn. And
he beyng made man/without sede of mā/hath cō
mytted vnto vs his godhed.   The Chapter.

IN all thynges haue I sought reste / & shall
dwell in the herytage of the lorde. Thē the
creatour of all thynges sayde/& cōmaunded me:
& he that hath created me/hathe rested in my ta=
bernacle. Thakes be to god. The antem. Hayle
Mary full of grace/the lorde is with the. Hayle
Mary full of grace the lorde is with the. Vers.
Blyssed be thou amonge women/and blyssed be
the fruyte of thy wombe. Our lorde is with the.

Glozy be to the father/to the sone / ⁊ to the holy ghost. Ayle mary full of grace our lozde is with the. Oly mother of god ⁊ virgyn perpetuall. Pray for vs to the lozde celestiall. Lozde god heare my prayer. And gyue hearynge vnto my clamour.

Raunt (we beseche the lozde god) that thy seruauntes maye Ioye contynuall healthe of body and soule/and throughe the gracyous intercessyon of the virgyn thy mother that we may be delyuered from this present heuynes and to haue the fruycyon of eternall gladnesse. By chzyst our lozde. So be it.

The spzite houre/in the moz>nyng early
To theyr iudge/called Pylate the Iues
Iesus with his handes bounden they cary
Whhere many a false wytnesse dyd hym accuse
In the necke they hym smyt/his body they bzuse
They spyt and defyled there is godly face
The lyght of heuyn/replete with all grace.
We worshyppe the Chzyste/with prayse ⁊ bendiccyon. Foz thou redemyddest the worlde from all afflyccyon.

Lozde Iesu Chzyste / sone of the lyuynge god/set thy holy passyon/crosse:and death betwene thy iudgement and our soules / both now and at the houre of death. And mozeouer vouchsaufe to graunt vnto the lyuynge / mercy and grace/to the deade pardon and rest / to thy holy Churche/peace and concozde/⁊ to vs poole

synners lyfe and ioye euerlastynge. Whiche lyuest and reygnest god with the father/& the holy
ghost/worlde without ende. So be it.

¶ The gloryous passyon of our lorde Jesu Chryst
delyuer vs from sorowfull heuynesse; and bryng
vs to the ioyes of paradyse. So be it.

¶ The first houre of the compassyon of oure Lady

Hen our lady in the mornyng behelde
Her only sone scourged & foule arayde
Bobbed/knocte/& his face with spytte defyled
God wote in hert/she was full sore dismayde
But yet alas it maketh myne herte afrayde
To thynke how she fell in greuous wepynge
And how dulfully her handes she gan wrynge

The verse. We do prayse the: and do pray the
mother of god moost mercyfull. The answere.
That thou entende / vs to defende/from death
that is moost sorowfull. The prayer.

Oly lorde Jesu / sone of the mooste swete
virgyn Mary / whiche sufferedest deathe
for vs vpō a Crosse/shew vnto vs thy mercy and
graūt vnto vs / & vnto all that deuoutly haue in
remēbraunce the cōpassyon of thy moost holy mo-
ther(for her sake)prosperous lyfe in this present
worlde/and throughe thy grace / eternall glorye
in the worlde to come. Wherin thou doest lyue &
reygne one god with the holy ghoste / worlde
without ende. So be it.

The dolourous cōpassyō of goddes moost swete
mother/brynge vs to the blysse of almyghty god
the father. So be it. The thyrde houre.

O God bende thy selfe in to my helpe.
Lorde haste the to helpe me.
Glorye be to the father/to the sone/&
to the holye ghoste.
As it was in the begynnynge as it
is nowe and euer shall be. So be it.
Ome holy ghost/O creatour eternall
In our myndes/to make visytacyon
And fulfyll thou with grace supernall.

Our hertes that be of thy creacyon
Remembre lorde author of saluacyon
That somtyme of a virgyn pure
Without helpe of mannes operacyon
Thou tokest vpon the our frayle nature.
O virgyn Mary moost gracyous
O mother of mercy incomparable
From our enemye defende thou vs
And in the houre of death be fauourable.
Glory to the lorde of myghtes moost
That of a virgyn chaste was bore
Glory to the father and the holy ghost
To them be praysyng for euermore. So be it.

When thou wast borne.

Ad dūm cum tribularer. The .cxix. Psalme.

I Cryed vnto the lorde when I was in trou:
ble/and he herde me.

O lorde delyuer my soule from lyenge lyppes: &
a deceytfull tonge.

What may be gyuen the:or what may be layde
agaynst the:to a deceytfull tonge.

The sharpe arrowes of the myghtye:with hotte
sparkelynge cooles.

Who is me for my restynge place is prolonged:
I haue dwelled with the inhabytātes of Cedar/
my soule was longe in exyle.

I was peasyble with the that hated peace:when
I spake vnto them/they assaulted me causeles.

Glory be to the father/to the sone/and to the ho
ly ghoste.

As it was in the begynnynge/as it is now and

oly mother of god/and virgyn perpetuall.
¶The verse. After thy byzth virgyn thou dydest
remayne. ¶The answere. praye to thy sone to sa
ue vs from payne.

Lozde god heare my prayer. And gyue hearyng
vnto my clamour. ¶The prayer.

Raunt (we beseche the lozde god) that thy
seruauntes maye Joye contynuall healthe
of body and soule/and throughe the gracyous in
tercessyon of the virgyn thy mother that we may
be delyuered frō this present heuynes and to ha
ue the fruycyon of eternall gladnesse. By Chzyst
our lozde. So be it. Blesse we the lozde. Thanke
we god. ¶The thyzde houre saythe thus

Boute thze houres after the sonne gan
sprynge
All the Jewes crye/Jesu to crucifye
And i scozne they hi clothed w purple clothynge
And in stede of a crowne/on his heade they tye
A crowne of thozne that pzycked cruelly
And lad hym fozth to the place where he dyed
With a great huge crosse on his shulders leyde
¶The verse We wozshyp the Chzyst with prayse
and benediccyon. ¶The answere. Foz thou rede
mydest the wozlde frō all afflicyon. ¶Let vs pray

Lozde Jesu Chzyst/sone of the lyuynge god
set thy holy passyon/Crosse: and death be
twene thy iudgement and our soules/both now
and at the houre of death. And mozeouer vouch
saufe to graunt vnto the lyuyng/mercy & grace/
to the deade pardon and rest/to thy holy Churche

D i

peace and concozde/and to vs pooze synners/lyfe
and ioye euerlastynge. Whiche lyuest & reygnest
god with the father/and the holy ghost / wozlde
without ende. So be it.

The glozyous passyon of our lozde Iesu Chzyst
delyuer vs frõ sozowfull heuynesse/and bzynge
vs to the ioyes of paradyse. So be it.

The nynthe houre of the compassyon of our lady

WHen the birgyn of birgyns behelde her so
About. iij. houres after the day gã sprig
With a sharpe crowne of thozne on his heade
done. And a great crosse on his shulders beryng
To the place of death the Iewes hym leadyng
Alas foz wo/downe in the strete she fell With as
sad an hert/as euer tonge coulde tell. The verse.
We do playse the / & do pray the ~~mother of~~ god
moost mercyfull. The Answere.
That thou entende/vs to defende / from death
that is moost sozowfull.   The prayer.

HOly lozde iesu/sone of the mooste swete bir=
gyn Mary / whiche suffredest deathe foz
vs vpõ a Crosse/shew vnto vs thy mercy & graũt
vnto vs / & vnto all that deuoutly haue in remẽ=
bzaunce the cõpassyon of thy ~~moost holy mother~~
(foz her sake) prosperous lyfe i this psent wozlde
& throughe thy grace/eternall glozye i ÿ wozlde
to come. wherin ÿ doest lyue & reygne one god w̃
the holy ghoste/wozlde without ende. So be it.
The dolourous cõpassyõ of goddes moost swete
mother/bzynge vs to the blysse of almyghty god
the father. So be it.   The syxte houre.

O God bende thy selfe in to my helpe.
Lorde haste the to helpe me.
Glory be to the father/to the sone/
and to the holye ghoste.
As it was in the begynnyng/as it
is nowe and euer shall be. So be it.
Prayse ye the lorde.   Veni creator.
Ome holy spiryte/O creatour eternall
In our myndes to make visytacyon

D ij

And fulfyll thou with grace supernall
Our hertes that be of thy creacyon
Remembre lorde author of saluacyon
That somtyme of a virgyn pure
Withhout helpe of mannes operacyon
Thou tokest vpon the our frayle nature
O virgyn Mary moost gracyous
O mother of mercy incomparable
From our enemye defende thou vs
And in the houre of death be fauourable.
Glory to the lorde of myghtes moost
That of a virgyn chaste was bore
Glory to the father and the holy ghost
To them be praysyng for euermore. So be it.
The antheme. The busshe that Moyses.
Ad te leuaui oculos. The .cxxi. Psalme.

Nto the haue I lyfte vp myne eyes o god:
whiche inhabytest the heuyns.
Euyn lyke as the eyes of seruautes wayt at the
handes of theyr maysters.
As the eyes of a handemayden be vpon her may=
sters: euyn so be our eyes vpon oure lorde god: vn
tyll he haue mercy on vs.
Haue mercy on vs/o lorde haue mercy on vs: for
we are fulfylled with moche contempte.
For our soule is fylled verye moche: beynge scor
ned of the ryche and dispysed of the proude.
Glory be to the father/to the sone/and to the ho=
lye ghoste.
As it was in the begynnyng: as it is nowe and
euer shall be. So be it.

Nisi quia dominus. ❧

Except the lorde had ben amonge vs (let Is
rael now speake) except the lorde had ben
amonge vs.

When men rose agaynst vs: perauenture they
myght haue swalowed vs vp quycke.

When theyr fury was great agaynst vs: perauē
ture water mought haue souped vs vp.

Our soule hath passed ouer a ryuer: our soule per
auenture myght haue passed ouer a water in
tollerable.

Blessed be the lorde/whiche hath not suffred vs
to be caught with theyr teeth.

Our soule hath ben delyuered/euyn as a sparowe
from the foulers snare.

The snare is worne out: and we are delyuered.

Our helpe consysteth in the name of the lorde:
whiche made heuyn and earth.

Glory be to the father/to the sone/and to the ho
lye ghoste.

As it was in the begynnynge/as it is now. and
euer shall be. So be it.

Qui confidunt.

They that truste in the lorde as a mountay
ne of Syō: he shall neuer be moued/which
inhabyteth Hierusalem.

Mountaynes are in the cyrcute of it/and the lorde
is in the cyrcuyt of his people: frō this tyme forth
and euermore.

For the lorde shall not leaue the rodde of syn
ners vpō the lotte of the iuste: leest the iuste shuld

H iij

extende theyr handes vnto synne.

o wel (o lorde) to the good and vpght in hert.

ut those that swarue: the lorde shall bryng in to bondes with them that worke wyckednesse: peace be vpon Israel.

lory be to the father/to the sone/and to the holy ghoste.

s it was in the begynnyng : as it is now/and euer shall be. So be it.

The Antheme.

he busshe that Moyses sawe preserued from burnyng (when it was vpon a lyght fyre) dyd sygnyfye to vs thy moost commendable virginite: goddes mother pray for vs.

The Chapter.

Nd so in Syon was I setled/and i the sanctifyed cyte also I rested: and in Hierusalē was my power. Thanke we god. The answere.

fter thy byrth vyrgyn thou dydest remayne.

After thy byrth vyrgyn thou dydest remayne.

The verse. ꝑay to thy sone to saue vs from payne. Virgyn thou dydest remayne. lory be to the father/to the sone/and to the holye ghoste. After thy byrth virgyn thou dydest remayne.

The verse. hou arte made beautefull and amorous. The answere. mother of god moost gloryous. lorde god heare my prayer. And gyue hearynge vnto my clamour. Let vs pray.

Raunt (we beseche the lorde god) that thy seruauntes may enioye contynuall healthe of body and soule/and throughe the gracyous intercessyon of the virgyn thy mother that we may

be delyuered frō this pzefent heuynes and to ha=
ue the fruycyon of eternall gladnesse. By Chzyst
our lozde. So be it. Blesse we the lozde. Thanke
we god.

¶ The fyze houre of the Crosse.

THe syzte houre spzyngynge befoze the
mydday
Jesu hande and foote to the crosse they nayled
Uuith the shamefullest deathe that they contry=
ue may
And in dispyte betwene two theues hym hanged
Uuhen they thought foz payn/that he tursted
His thurst foz to quenche they pzofered hym gal
This lambe so illuded bought our synnes all.
The verse. we wozshyp the Chzyst with pzayse
benediccyō. The answere. Foz thou redempdest
the wozlde from all afflyccyon.

¶ The prayer.

LOzde Jesu Chzyst/sone of the lyuynge god
set thy holy passyon/Crosse: dath betwe=
ne thy indgement and our soules/both now and
at the houre of death. And mozeouer vouchsaufe
to graunt vnto the lyuyng/mercy grace/to the
deade pardon rest/to thy holy Churche/peace
concozde/and to vs pooze synners /lyfe and ioye
euerlastynge. Uuhiche lyuest and reygnest god
with the father/and the holy ghost/wozlde with
out ende. So be it.

The glozyous passyon of our lozde Jesu Chzyst
delyuer vs from sozowfull heuynesse: and bzyng

H iiij

vs to the ioyes of paradyse. So be it.

The fyrte houre of the compallyin of our Lady.

His piteous mother befoꝛe the none tyde
Her sone eleuate on the croſſe myght ſe
His body toꝛne and wꝛapped with woūdes wyde
Haugynge betwene theues as ſhamefull as coulde be.
His thurſt to ſlacke/bytter gall taſted he
At her owne herte/his payne ſhe felt ſo ſoꝛe
She wayled and cryed a.ℂ.ſythe therfoꝛe.

The verſe. Aue do pꝛayſe the / ⁊ do pꝛay the mother of god mooſt mercyfull. The Anſwere.

That thou intende vs to defende / from deathe that is moſt ſoꝛowfull. The pꝛayer.

HOly loꝛde Jeſu/ſone of the mooſt ſwete virgyn Mary / whiche ſuffered death foꝛ vs vpon a croſſe/ſhewe vnto vs thy mercy ⁊ graunt vnto vs/and vnto all that deuoutely haue in remembꝛaunce the compaſſyon of thꝭ mooſt holy mother(foꝛ her ſake)pꝛoſperous lyfe in this pꝛeſent woꝛlde / and thꝛoughe thy grace eternall gloꝛye in the woꝛlde to come. Wherin thou dooſt lyue and reygne one god / with the holy ghoſt/woꝛlde without ende.

So be it.
The doloꝛous cõpaſſyõ of goddꝭ mooſte ſwete mother/bꝛynge vs to the bleſſe of almyghty god the father. So be it.

The nynth houre of our Lady.

God bende thy selfe in to my helpe.
Lorde haste the to helpe me.
Glory be to the father/to the sone/
and to the holye ghoste.
As it was in the begynnyng/as it
is nowe and euer shall be. So be it.
Prayse ye the lorde. Hymne. Veni creator.
Ome holy spiryte/O creatour eternall
In our myndes to make vysytacyon

And fulfyll thou with grace supernall
Our hertes that be of thy creacyon
Remembre lorde author of saluacyon
That somtyme of a virgyn pure
Without helpe of mannes operacyon
Thou tokest vpon the our frayle nature

Virgyn Mary moost gracyous
O mother of mercy incomparable
From our enemye defende thou vs
And in the houre of death be fauourable.
Glory to the lorde of myghtes moost
That of a virgyn chaste was bore
Glory to the father and the holy ghost
To them be praysyng for euermore. So be it.

The Antheme. The roote of Jesse.
In conuertendo. The .cxxvi. Psalme.

When the lorde tourned the captyuyte of
Syon: we were made gladde.
Then was our mouthe fulfylled with myrth : &
our tongue with ioyfulnesse.
Then shal they say amonge the gentylles : the
lorde hath done greatly for them.
The lorde hathe done greatly for vs: we are ma=
de ioyfull.
Lorde conuerte our captyuyte: as a ryuer in the
southe.
They that sowe with teres : shall reape with
gladnes.
They goynge forth went and wepte castynge
theyr sedes.
But comynge agayne they shall come with ioye

bearynge theyr handes full of corne.

Glory be to the father/to the sone/and to the holy ghoste.

As it was in the begynnynge/as it is now and euer shall be. So be it.

Nisi dominus edificauerit.

Excepte the lorde haue buylded the house: they haue labored in vayn which buylde it Oneles the lorde haue kepte the cyte : he hath watched in vayne that kepeth it.

It is in vayn for you to ryse before lyght : aryse after your syttyng:ye that eat the bred of sorow.

When he hath gyuen slepe to his welbeloued lo the herytage of the lorde is chyldren:the rewarde is the fruyte of the wombe.

As arowes in the hande of the myghty:so be the chyldren of smyters.

Blessed is the man : whiche fulfylled his despre of them:he shall not be confounded whē he shall speake to his enemyes in the gate.

Glory be to the father/to ẏ sone/& to ẏ holy ghost.

As it was in the begynnynge/as it is now and euer shall be. So be it.

Beati omnes.

Blessed be all that feare the lorde : whiche walketh in his wayes.

For thou shalt eate the labours of thyne handes:thou shalt be blessed/and wel shalt thou be.

Thy wyfe shall be as a plenteous vyne:in the sydes of thyne house.

Thy sones lyke the plantes of Olyue trees: all

aboute thy table.

Lo/thus shall a man be blessed/whiche feareth the lorde.

The lorde of Syon blesse the:and thou shalte se the goodes of Hierusalē al the dayes of thy lyfe.

And thou shalte se the chyldren of thy chyldren:and peace vpon Israel.

Glory be to the father/to the sone/and to the.&c.

As it was in the begynnynge/as it is now and euer shall be.So be it.

The Anthem. The roote of Jesse hath borne buddes:a starre is rysyn out of the house of iacob a virgyn hathe borne the sauyoure of the worlde we prayse the lorde god. The Chapter.

And I haue planted my roote in an honourable nacyon/whose inherytaūce is in the partes of my god/& amōge the cōpany of sayntes is my taryenge.Thākes be to god.The answere. Thou art made beauteful & amorous. Thou art made beauteful & amourous. The verse. O mother of god moost glorious.And amourous. Glory be to the father/to the sone/& to the holy ghost Thou arte made beauteful and amorous. versk. Graūt me blessed lady to auāsce the with glorye The answere. Agaynst thyne enemyes gyue me the vyctory. Lorde god heare my prayer.And gyue hearynge vnto my clamour. Let vs praye.

Graunt (we beseche the lorde god) that thy seruauntes may enioye contynuall healthe of body & soule / & throughe thy gracyous intercessyon of the virgyn thy mother that we may be

delyuered frõ this present heuynes & to haue the
frupcyõ of eternall gladnesse. By chryst our lorde
So be it. Blesse we the lorde. Thanke we god.

The syxth houre of the crosse.

Ur mercyfull lorde Jesu goddes sone
Callynge vnto his father almyghty
Yelded vp his soule/and full vpon none
The spyryte departed that blessed body
The sonne waxed darke / the earthe quoke won=
dersly. Great wõders thynges to beholde & heare
And yet a knyght perseð his hert with a spere.
The verse. we worshyp the Chryst with prayse &
benediccyõ. The answere. For thou redemydest
the worlde from al afflyccyon. Let vs pray.

LOrde Jesu Chryst/sone of the lyuynge god
set thy holy passyon/Crosse:& death betwe=
ne thy iudgement and our soules/both now and
at the houre of death. And moreouer vouchsaufe
to graunt vnto the lyuyng/mercy & grace/to the
deade pardon & rest/to thy holy Churche/peace &
concorde/and to vs poore synners / lyfe and ioye
euerlastynge. Whiche lyuest and reygnest god
with the father/and the holy ghost/worlde with
out ende. So be it.

The gloryous passyõ of our lorde Jesu chryst.

The nynthe houre of the crucyfyd of our lady.

SOone after noone this mother soreweping
Her sone/callynge to his father myght hea
re. Sawe from the body/the soule departynge
And a knyght openynge his hert with a spere
For sorowe/she fell downe in a sowne there

O mercyfull lorde god/what earthly wyght
Wolde not haue rewed of that pyteous syghte.
The verse. We do prayse the : and do pray the
mother of god moost mercyfull. The answere.
That thou entende / vs to defende/from death
that is moost sorowfull. The prayer.

Oly lorde Iesu / sone of the mooste swete
virgyn Mary / whiche sufferedest deathe
for vs vpō a Crosse/shew vnto vs thy mercy and
graūt vnto vs / & vnto all that deuoutly haue in
remēbraunce the cōpassyon of thy moost holy mo
ther(for her sake)prosperous lyfe in this present
worlde/and throughe thy grace / eternall glorye
in the worlde to come. Wherin thou doest lyue &
reygne one god with the holy ghoste / worlde
without ende. So be it.
The dolourous cōpassyō of goddes moost swete
mother/brynge vs to the blysse of almyghty god
the father. So be it.

What is ment by this worde Euynsonge.
Yke as the seruyce that we be dayly accu=
stomed to say i the mornynge is called ma=
tyns/euyn so is the seruyce vsed to be sayde or sō
ge towarde euyn/called Euynsonge. And this is
the true sygnifycacyon and meanynge of the sa=
me worlde/whiche we call Euynsonge of our La=
dy/bycause it is specyally done in the laude and
praysynge of her.

The Euynsonge of our Lady.

God bende thy selfe in to my helpe.
Lorde haste the to helpe me.
Glory be to the father/to the sone / ♄
to the holy ghoste.

As it was in the begynnynge / as it
is now and euer shall be. So be it.

After the byrth.

Letatus sum.

The Euynsonge.

I Reioysed in those thynges that were sayde to me:we shall go in to the lordes house.

Oure feete were standynge in thy gates:O Hierusalem.

Hierusalem whiche is buylded lyke a cytie:whose perticypacyon is within it selfe.

For thyther ascended the trybes / euyn the trybes of the lorde : the testymonye of Israel to acknowledge the lordees name.

For there sate the sytters in iudgement : euyn the seate of the house of Dauid.

Pray ye for the peace of Hierusalem : and they shall haue plentye that loue the.

Let peace be made throughe thy vertue:& plenteousnes in thy houses.

For my brothers and kynredes sakes:I prayed peace for the.

For the house of our lorde god:I besought good thynges for the.

Glory be to the father/to the sone/and to the holy ghoste.

As it was in the begynnynge/as it is now and euer shall be.So be it.

Ad te leuaui oculos. The .CXX. Psalme.

UNto the haue I lyfte vp myne eyes o god: whiche inhabytest the heuyns.

Euyn lyke as the eyes of seruautes wayt at the handes of theyr maysters.

As the eyes of a handemayden be vpon her maysters:euyn so be our eyes vpon oure lorde god: vntyl he haue mercy on vs.

Shal treble and quake:befoze the face of the
when thou shalt come:in thy most feruent yze
The woılde to iudge/by hotte burnynge fyze.
        Wherfoze good loide/we humbly
the requyze.
That of thy goodnes thou woldeſt not foiget
To delyuer me/from euerlaſtynge fyze
whiche blakeſt vp the blaſen gates great
And vplyfted haſt the lowe infernall ſeate
And vnto lyght/them dydeſt reſtoze
whiche in payne of darkeneſſe/hadde ben longe
befoze.
whiche vnto the thus dyd call and cry
welcome to vs our blyſſed ſauyour ſwete
welcome our redemer/welcome hertely
whiche blakeſt vp the blaſen gates great
And viſited haſt the lowe infernall ſeate
And vnto lyght/them dydeſt reſtoze
whiche in payne of darkeneſſe hadde ben longe
befoze.   Reſte in peace.
Soue it.   y bzouſed.
   iſere mei deus.
   Aue mercy vpon me (o god) accoıdynge to
    thy great mercy.
  nd accoıdyng to the multitude of thy cōpaſ-
ſyons:wype away myn iniquite.
Yet waſſhe me moze from myne iniquite:& clenſe
me moze from my ſynne.
Foz J knowledge myne iniquite:and my ſynne
is euer befoze myne eyes.
  gaynſt the onely haue J ſynned / and haue

done euyll in thy syght:that thou mayste be iusti=
stifyed in thy wordes/& mayst vaynquysshe whē
thou hast iudged.

Lo I was begotten in wyckednesse/and my mo
ther concepued me in synne.

Lo thou haste loued trueth / the vnknowē and
secrete thynges of thy wysdome hast thou reue=
led vnto me.

Spryncle me lorde with ysope/and so shall I be
cleane/thou shalt wasshe me/and then shal I be
whyter then snowe.

Vnto my hearynge shalt thou gyue ioye & glad=
nesse:and my brosed bones shalbe refresshed.

Tourne thy face frō my synnes:and wype away
all my wyckednesse.

A pure herte create in me (oh god) and an vp
ryght spyryte renewe within me.

Cast me not away from thy face:and thyne holy
spyryte take not from me.

Take me agayn to reioyse in thy sauynge helth
and strengthen me with a pryncypal spiryte.

I wyll istruct the wycked in thy wayes: and the
vngodly shall be conuerted vnto the.

Delyuer me from bloudes (oh god) the god of
my health : and my tonge shal exalte thy ryght=
wysenesse.

Lorde open thou my lyppes / and my mouthe
shall pronounce thy prayse.

For yf thou haddest desyred sacryfices/I hadde
surely gyuen it/ but thou delytest not in burnt
offrynges.

A sacryfyce to god is a lowly spirit: a contrite &
an humble herte dispyce not (o god)

Deale gētly of thy fauourable beneuolēce with
Syon: that the walles of Hierusalē may be buyl=
te agayne.

Then shalt thou accept the sacryfyce of ryght=
wysenesse: oblacyons and burnte offerynges/thē
shall they lay calues vpon thyne altare.

Lorde gyue them eternall reste: and let conty=
nuall lyght shyne vnto them.

The antheme. My broused bones lorde shall be
refresshed. The antheme. Heare lorde.

Te decet hymnus. The lxiiij. Psalme.

Prayse becōmeth the (o god) i Syō: & let eue=
ry pmyse be pfourmed to the in hierusalē.

O god heare my prayer: vnto þ shall euery crea=
ture come.

The wordes of the wycked haue preuayled a=
gaynste vs: & vnto our vngodlynes: thou shalte
be mercyfull.

Blessed is he/whome thou haste chosen and ta=
ken vp: he shall dwell in thy court.

He shal be satisfied with the godes of thy hous
holy is thy temple/ and meruaylous in equite.

Heare vs/o god our sauyour: the hope of all the
costes of the earth/ and mayne see.

Thou preparest the hylles with thy strength:
whiche beynge gyrded with power/ styrest the
depnes of the see: the rorynge waters therof.

People shalbe affrayde/ & they that dwel vpon
the see costes/ shall drede thy sygnes: thou shalt

P ij

refreſſhe the moznynge and euenyng fruyt es.

Thou haſte viſyted the earth/and haſt watered it:thou haſt done moche to enryche it.

The flode of god is replenyſſhed with waters: thou haſt pzepared theyz fode/foz ſo is the pzepa racyon of it.

Thou encreaſynge the watercourſes of it / mul: tiplyeſt the spzynges of it with ſofte ſhowzes / it ſhall englad the out spzynges.

Thou ſhalte bleſſe the crowne of the yere of thy benygnyte/and thy felbes ſhal be replenyſſhed with habundaunce.

The goodly places of deſerte ſhal waxe flatte: & the lytell hylles ſhall be gyzte with gladnes.

The rammes of thy flocke are well fleced: & the valeys ſhall creaſe with weate:ye they ſhal out: crye and gyue pzayſe.

LOzde gyue the eternall reſte:and let cõtynuall lyght ſhyne vnto them.

The antheme.
Heare my pzayer / o lozde / vnto the ſhal euery creature come. The antheme He hath recevued.

Deus deus meus. The fiffte ſalme.
God thou arte my god: early do I watche after the.

My ſoule hath longed after the:my fleſſhe hath thyzſted very moche.

In to a countre deſerte wylde and dzye:ſo haue I appered befoze the I an holy place foz to ſe thy power and thy glozy.

Foz thy mercy is better thē lyfe:my lyppes ſhall pzayſe the.

So shal I prayse the in my lyfe/and in thy name I shall lyfte vp my handes.

My soule shall be satysfyed/as it were with enterlarde and fatnes/and my mouthe shall prayse the with lyppes full of ioye.

So haue I ben myndefull of the vpō my bed : in the mornyng tymes:bycause thou waste my helper/I shall let my thought on the.

And I shall reioyse vnder the couerte of thy wynges : my soule hath cleaued vnto the / thy ryght hande hath susteyne me.

They veryly haue sought my lyfe in vayne:they shall go in to the lower partes of the erth they shall be put ī to the power of a swerde:they shall be the parthes of foxes.

The kynge truely shall ioye in god / all shal be praysed that sweare in hym : for the mouthe of them that speake vngodlynes is stopped.

Deus misereatur nostri. The.lxvi.psalme.

God haue mercy vpon vs/and blesse vs: let hym shewe his face vnto vs/and haue mercy vpon vs.

That thy way may be knowen in the earth:and thy sauynge helth also amonge all nacyons.

Let thy people make knowledge vnto god:let all nacyons confesse the.

Ioyfull and glad be all folke:because thou rulest the people with equite:& ordrest nacyōs in earth.

People knowledge the to be god/let all nacyōs confesse the:for the earth hathe brought forth her fruyte.

P iij

Blesse vs our god / and all that inhabyte the earth:that al the partes therof may feare the.

Lorde gyue them eternall reste : and let contynuall lyght shyne vnto them.

The antheme. Lorde thy ryght hande hathe defended me. Antheme. From the gates of hell.

The songe of Ezachias. Esay the .xxxviij. Chapiter. Ego dixi in dimidio.

I Sayd in the myddes of my dayes:J shall go to the gates of hell.

J desyred the resydue of my yeres: J sayd to my selfe / J shal not se the lorde god in the lande of the lyuynge.

J shall not se man any moze : and hym that dwelleth in reste.

My generacyon is taken from me / and folden vp:as the shepherdes tente.

My lyfe is cut of lyke a weauers webbe : euyn when J began / he cutte me downe: frō moznyng vntyll the nyght thou shalt fynysshe me.

J was in hope vntyll moznynge:euyn as a lyon: so dyd he gnawe by bones.

Frō moznynge vntyll nyght thou shalte fynysshe me:as a yonge swalow / so shall J crye & shall muse as a doue.

Myne eyen daseled / with lokyng on hygh.

Lorde J am enfozced / answere foz me : what J shall say:oz what shall he answere me / syns J haue done it.

J shall reuolue all my yeres vnto the with great bytternes of herte.

Lorde yf they lyue thus:⁊ the lyfe of my spirite be i suche thynges/thou shalt correct me ⁊ quyc=
ken me:lo in peace my sorowe is most bytterest.

Thou surely haste delyuered my soule that it shulde not perysshe:thou haste cast behynde thy backe all my synnes.

Nor neyther hell shall knowledge the/nor death shall prayse the:they that discende in to the pyt/ shall not trust vpon thy veryte.

He that is lyuyng:the man lyuynge shal know= ledge the lyke as I do nowe:the father vnto the chyldren/shall declare thy trueth.

Saue me lorde/and we shall synge our psalmes in the lorde house/all the dayes of oure lyfe.

Lorde gyue them eternall reste : and let conty= nuall lyght shyne vnto them.

The antheme. From the gates of hell lorde de= lyuer theyr soules. Anthema. Euery spirite.

Laudate dnm de celis. The .cxlviij. Psalme.

Prayse ye the lorde of heuyns : prayse ye hym in the hygh places.

Prayse ye hym all his aungelles:all his powers prayse ye hym.

Prayse hym sonne and moone : all sterres and lyght prayse ye hym.

The hyghest of heuyns prayse ye hym : and the waters that are aboue the heuyns / lette them prayse the lordes name.

For by his worde all thynges were made:by his commaundement al thynges were created.

He hath stablysshed them euerlastyngly in the

worlde of worldes: he hathe set a lawe & it shall
not expyre.

Prayse the lorde ye dragons: and all depnesses
of the earth.

Fyre/hayle/snowe/yse/stormes/of wyndes:
that do his commaundement.

Mountaynes and all lytle hylles: woode bearyn=
ge fruyte and all ceder trees.

Beastes and all maner of catell: serpentes/and
fethered foules.

Kynges of the earth/& all people: prynces and
all iudges of the earth.

Bachelers and maydens/olde men and yong/let
them prayse the name of the lorde: for the name
of hym onely hath ben exalted.

The knowledge of hym is aboue heuyn & earth:
and he hathe exalted the horne of his people.

Prayse be vnto all his sayntes: to the sones of
Israel/to the people approchyng vnto hym.

Lorde gyue them eternall reste: & let contynuall
lyght shyne vnto them.

Cantate dño canticũ.

Synge we vnto the lorde a newe song: the
prayse of hym is in the congregacyon of
sayntes.

Let Israel reioyse in hym that made hym: & let
the sones of Syon tryumphe in theyr kynge.

Let them prayse his name with daunsyng: let
them synge vnto hym with tympany an harpe.

For the lorde is well pleased with his people: &
hath exalted the lowly in to saluacyon.

Ayntes shall tryumphe in glozye: theyz shall make ioye in theyz chambzes.

He prayses of god shall be in theyz mouthes & two edged swozdes in theyz handes.

To take vengeaunce amonge nacyons: and cozreccyons amonge people.

To bynde theyz kynges in fetters: and theyz nobles in manacles of pzon.

Oz to execute on them the iudgemẽt wzytten: this is glozye to all his sayntes.

Laudate dñm in sanctis.

Rayse the lozde in his sayntes: prayse hym in the fyzmament of his power.

Zayse hym in his strength: prayse hym accoz= dynge to the almyghtynes of his maiestye.

Zayse hym with the sounde of a trõpette: pray= se hym with harpe and lute.

Zayse hym with tympany & daunsynge: prayse hym with rebeckes and ozgans.

Zayse hym with clarysymballes well sõũdyng: prayse hym with symballes of swetnes let euery spirite prayse the lozde.

Ozde gyue thẽ eternall resse: and let cõtynuall lyght shyne vnto them. what soe= uer thynge is endued with spirite: let it prayse the lozde. From the gates of hell.

Lozde delyuer theyz soules.

I am. ¶

Lessed be þ lozde god of Israel: foz he hath visyted and redemed his people.

And hath reysed vp an hozne of saluacyõ vnto

vs:in the house of his seruaunt Dauyd.

Euyn as he pmysed by the mouthes of his holy
prophetes/whiche were syns the worlde began.

That we shulde be saued frõ our enemyes: and
from the handes of all that hate vs.

To fulfyll the mercy promysed to our fathers &
to remembre his holy couenaunt.

And to pfourme the othe/whiche he sware vn∣
to our father abraham that he wolde gyue vs.

That we beynge delyuered out of the handes of
our enemyes/myght serue hym without feare.

In holynes and ryghtwysnes before hym : all ye
dayes of our lyfe.

And thou chylde/shalte be called the prophet of
the hyest:for thou shalt go before the face of the
lorde to prepare his wayes.

And to gyue knowledge of saluacyon vnto his
people:for the remyssyon of synnes.

Through the tender mercy of our god / by the
which he spryngyng from an hye hath vifyted vs.

To gyue lyght to them that sate in darknesse &
in the shadowe of death:and to guyde oure feete
in to the way of peace.

Lorde gyue them eternall reste: and let conty∣
nuall lyghts shyne vnto them.

The Antheme. I am the resurreccyon and lyfe:
he that byleueth in me / ye all though he were
deade/yet shall he lyue: and who soeuer lyueth
and byleueth i me/shall not se euerlastyng death.
Lorde haue mercy on vs. Chryste haue mercy on
vs. Lorde haue mercy on vs. Our father. &c. And

leade vs not. But delyuer vs.

Exaltabo te domine.

I Shal exalte the (o lorde) for thou hast defen
ded me: neyther hast thou suffered myne ene
myes to haue theyr pleasure vpon me.

O lorde / my god / I haue cryed vnto the: & thou
hast healed me.

Lorde thou hast brought my soule out of the
lowe place: thou hast preserued me from thē that
descende in to the pytte.

Synge vnto the lorde we that be his sayntes: &
confesse ye the memory of his holynes.

For there is vengeaunce in his displeasure and
lyfe in his pleasure.

At the euenynge waylynge shall contynue: and
in the mornynge gladnes.

Veryly I sayd in my welthynes: I shall neuer
more be moued.

Lorde through thy good wyll thou hast lent
strength vnto my beautye.

Thou turnedst thy face from me: and I was all
astonyed.

Vnto the (lorde) shal I crye: and shal pray vnto
my god.

What profyte is there in my bloude / when I
shall discende in to corrupcyon.

Shall dust make knowledge vnto the or shal it
publysshe thy trouth.

The lorde hath herde / & hath had mercy on me:
the lorde is made myne helper.

Thou hast tourned my sorowe in to ioye: thou

haste cutte my sacke:& haste compassed me with
gladnes.

To the ende that my glory myght synge to the/
and myght not be pryckte:o my lorde god I shall
euermore confesse the.

Lorde gyue them eternall reste:& let contynuall
lyght shyne vnto them.

From the gates of hell. Lorde delyuer theyr sou=
les. I trust to se the goodes of the lorde. In the
lande of the lyuynge. Lorde heare my prayer. And
let my clamour come vnto the. ¶ The pray.

God whiche by the mouthe of saynt Paule
thyne apostle/haste taught vs/not to be so
ry for them that slepe in Chryste/graunt we bese
che the/that in the comynge of thy sonne our lor
de Iesu Chryste/we with all other faythfull peo
ple beyng departed/may be gracyously brought
vnto ioyes euerlastyng:which shalt come to iud=
ge the quycke & the deade/& the worlde by fyre.

Almyghty eternall god/to whome there is
neuer any prayer made without hope of
mercy/be propiciable to the soule of thy seruaunt
that seynge it departed from this lyfe in the
confessyon of thy name/thou wylte cause it to be
associate to the company of thy sayntes. By
Chryste our lorde.

God of whose mercy there is no nomble ad=
myt our prayers/for the soules of thy ser
uauntes the byshoppes. And graunte vnto them
the lande of pleasure and lyght/in the felawshyp
of thy blessed aungels. By Chryste our lorde.

The Dirige.

Ord enclyne thyn eare vnto our prayers wherin we ryght deuoutly call vpō thy mercy/that thou wylte bestowe the soules of thy seruauntes bothe mē & womē(whiche thou hast cōmaunded to depart from this worlde)in the cou̅tre of peace and reste/and further/cause them to be made parteyners with thy sayntes. By Chryste our lorde.

W e beseche the lorde that the prayer of thy supplyautes may auayle to the soules of thy seruautes of eyther kynde/that thou wylte bothe pourge thē of all theyr synnes & cause thē to be partakers of thy redēpcyon.whiche lyuest & reygnest god/worlde without ende.So be it.

This psalme folowyng is to be sayd in tyme of tribulacyon and daūger.

U oce mea ad dn̄m clamaui. The.crli.Psalme.

W Ith my voyce vnto the lorde I haue cryed : with my voyce I haue prayed to the lorde.

I vtter my prayer in the syght of hym : and my trouble before hym I declare.

Yea and that vntyl my breath fayled me: & thou hast knowen my wayes.

In the same waye that I walked:the proude haue hydden a snare for me.

I loked vpon my ryght hande & sawe:and there was none that wolde knowe me.

Refuge is taken frō me:an there is none that requyreth my soule.

I haue cryed vnto the (o lorde) I haue sayde : þ

arte my hope : my porcyon in the lande of the ly=
uynge.

Intende vnto my prayer : for I am brought
passynge lowe.

Delyuer me from them that persecute me : for
they are made very stronge agaynst me.

Delyuer my soule out of pryson to confesse thy
name: the ryghtuous loke after me / vntyl that
thou requyte me.

THe holy and indiuisible Trinyte:to the hu
manyte of Iesu chryst crucyfyed/glory infy
nite be gyuen of euery creature/ worlde without
ende.So be it.

Blessed be the swete name of our lorde Iesu
Chryste:& of the gloryous virgyn Mary his mo=
ther for euermore.

And the soules of all true beleuers/beynge de=
parted through the mercy of god/ may reste i pea
ce.So be it.

Praysynge be to god/peace to the lyuynge/and
rest vnto the deade.So be it.

¶The argument of the commendacyons.

a good argument fyt for the frynds

THis psalme folowynge/accordynge to the
nombre of the hebrew letters is diuided in
to.xxij.Chapiters/which are called Octonaries:
bycause euery of thē cōteyneth eyght bles.But
why is it called the cōmendacyons of soules / I
moche meruayle:for yf they meane it of the sou=
les departed/then after my iudgement do they

gretly erre/namely syns it is/noz can not other=
wyse be applyed/but eyther as a spirytuall medi=
tacion of the ryghteous in the lawes of god: oz
els to be the voyce of those blessed soules/ which
beynge rysen with Chzyste in a newnes of lyfe/do
cotynually crye and cal vpon hym/ to be enstru=
cted and lyue after his wozde and commaunde=
ment. Foz the vnderstandynge wherof two thyu
ges are to be noted. The one / that we do make
therin a feruent & herty peticyon vnto god / that
he vouchesafe to teache /dyzecte and guyde vs
in the waye of iustyce and veryte. The other /
that in all poyntes touchynge our saluacyon/we
shulde in no wyse cleaue to the doctrynes oz p=
suacions of men. And therfoze is the hole psalme
garnysshed with these wozdes (thy law thy wa=
yes/thy pzeceptes/thy iudgementes / and suche
lyke)whiche glyster euery where: lyke to bzyght
and radyant sterres/as who shulde say that all
the lawes/wayes/and iudgementes of men are
fallyble/and therfoze not to be folowed. Also it
is a complaynt of the godly congregacyou / ex=
pzessynge howe soze it greueth them to se the
lawes of god reiected and set at nought/& man=
nes wayes and inuencions to be receyued in stea
de therof:pzonunsynge them onely to be blessed/
whiche walke in the waye of the lozde / and are
hooly gyuen to serche his lawe / beynge nyghte
and daye earnestly occupyed in diuine studyes.
To al suche doeth his Psalmes gyue hyghe and
synguler commendacyons.

Commendacyons.

Beati immaculati.   The .crit. Psalme.

Blessed are they that be vnspotted: whiche walke in the lawe of the lorde.

Blessed are they that serche his testymonies: that seke hym with all theyr herte.

For they truely which worke wyckedly haue not walked i his wayes.

Thou haste cōmaunded thy commaundementes to be kept very streytly.

Wolde to god my wayes myght be dyrected to kepe thy iustyfycacyons.

Then shall I not be confounded: when I shall be well sene in all thy commaundementes.

I shall acknowledge the dyrectly in my herte: in that that I haue lerned the iudgementes of thy ryghtuous.

I shal kepe the iustyfycacyons: thou shalte not forsake me at not tyme.

Werin doeth the yonge mā correcte his lyfe: in kepynge of thy commaundementes.

With all my herte I haue sought the out: put me not away from thy commaundementes.

In my herte I haue hydde thy wordes that I myght not offende the.

O lorde thou arte blessed: teache me thy iustyfycacyons.

With my lyppes I haue pronūced all the iudgementes of thy mouthe.

I haue ben delyted in the way of thy testymo:

nies/as it were in all maner of ryches.

shall be exercised in thy commaundementes/ and I shall consyder thy wayes.

shall study in thy iustifycacyōs: I shall not forget thy wordes.

Rewarde thy seruaunt: quycken me and I shall kepe thy wordes.

Open myne eys / and I shall consydre the mercyaulousnes of thy lawe.

am a straūger in the lande/hyde not from me thy commaundementes.

My soule hath desyred thy iustyfycacyon in all tymes.

Thou hast rebuked the proud men: cursed are they/whiche declyne from thy commaūdemētes.

Take from me opprobry and contempte: for I haue sought after thy commaundementes.

And truely the prynces haue bē set agaynst me/ and they spake agaynst me: but thy seruaūt was styll exercysed in thy iustyfycacyons.

For thy testymonies are my meditacyon: thy iustyfycacyons is my counsell.

My soule hathe cleaued to the groūde/quycken me accordyng to thy worde.

haue shewed my wayes/and thou hast herde me: teache me thy iustyfycacyons.

Instructe me in the way of thy iustyfycacyons: and I shall be exercised in thy meruayles.

My soule hath slepte for werynes: confyrme me in thy wordes.

Remeue from me the way of iiquite/and accor:

Q i

dynge to thy lawe haue mercy on me.

I haue chosen the way of trueth: I haue not for=
gotten thy iudgementes.

I haue cleaued to thy testimonies: put me not to
confucyon.

I haue ronne the waye of thy commaundemen=
tes/when thou hast eased my herte.

Good lorde set the waye of thy iustyfyca=
cyons to me for a lawe: and I wyll euer seke
it out.

Gyue vnto me vnderstandynge/ I shall serche
thy lawe: and shall kepe the same with myne ho=
le herte.

Leade me in the patthe of thy commaundemen=
tes/for I haue wysshed the same.

Inclyne my herte in to thy testymonies: and not
in to couetyse.

Tourne away myne eyes/that they se not vani=
te: quycken me in thy way.

Ordre thy worde to thy seruaunt in thy feare.

Cut of myne opprobrye/whiche I suspected: for
thy iudgementes be ioyous.

Lo I haue desyred thy commaundementes: in
thy equite quycken me.

And let thy mercy come vpon me/o lorde &
thy health accordynge to thy promyse.

And I shal answere to them that vpbraydeme
with checkes: for I haue trusted in thy wordes.

And take not the worde of trueth frō my mouth
on no parte: for I haue moche trusted in thy iud=
gementes.

And I shall kepe thy lawe in the worlde/and in
to the worlde of worldes.

And I haue walked at large:for I haue sought
thy commaundementes.

And I spake of thy testymonies in the syght of
kynges:and I was not confounded.

And I shall be occupied in thy cōmaundemen=
tes/whiche I haue loued.

And I haue lyfte vp my handes to thy cōmaun
dementes/whiche I haue loued:and I shall be
occupyed in thy iustyfycacyons.

REmembre thy worde to thy seruaunt:in
whiche thou hast gyuen me hope.

The same hath cōforted me in my humylyte for
thy worlde hath quyckened me.

The proude men haue done wyckednes on eue=
ry syde:but I haue not declyned from thy lawe.

I haue ben myndeful of thy iudgementes good
lorde/frō the begynnynge of the worlde:and ha=
ue ben conforted.

Defaulte hath holdē me bycause of synners:for=
sakynge thy lawe.

Thy iustifycacyons were to me songes/i the pla=
ce of my wayfaryinge.

I haue ben myndefull in the nyght of thy name
good lorde:and I haue kepte thy lawe.

This was done to me/forbycause I serched out
thy iustyfycacyons.

O Lorde thou arte my porcyon:I haue promy
sed to kepe thy lawe.

I haue prayed before thy face with al my hert
Q ij

haue mercy on me accordynge to thy promyse.

I haue confydered my wayes:and I haue couerted my fote in to thy testymonies.

I was redy:and I was not troubled:but that I myght kepe thy commaundementes.

The cordes of synners haue bewrapt me/and I haue not forgoten thy lawe.

I rose vp in the myndes of the nyght/that I myght acknoweledge the:vpon the iudgemētes of thy iustyfycacyons.

I am a parttaker of all that feare the:& of them that kepe thy commaundementes.

O lorde the earth is full of thy mercye:teache me thy iustifycacyons.

Thou hast delt gentilly with thy seruaunt good lorde/accordynge to thy worde.

Teache me goodnes/lernynge and knowledge: for I haue beleued thy commaundementes.

I haue synned befor̄e I was humble:therfore I haue kepte thy worde.

Thou arte good/and in thy goodnes teache me thy iustyfycacyons.

The iniquite of proude men is multyplied vpon me:but I with all my hole herte shall searche out thy commaundementes.

My hert is congyled lyke mylke: I truly haue thought vpon thy commaundementes.

It was good to me that thou dydest brynge me lowe that I myght lerne thy iustifycacyons.

The lawe of thy mouthe is good to me:& a boue a myllyon of golde or syluer.

Hy hādes haue made me and fourmed mē: gpue me vnderstandynge that J may ler= ne thy commaundementes.

They that feare the shall se me/¢ shall be glad: for J haue trusted moche in thy.wordes.

I haue knowen lorde that thy iudgementes are equite:and i thy trueth thou haste humiliate me.

Let thy mercy be shewed/that it may cōfort me/ accordyng to thy promyse/which am thy seruaūt

Let thy mercyes come to me/¢ J shal lyue:for thy lawe is my meditacyon.

Let the proude whiche wrongfully haue done wyckednes vnto me/be cōfounded:and J truely shall be exercised in thy commaundementes.

Let them be conuerted to me/whiche feare the: and they that knowe thy testymonies.

Let my herte be imaculate in thy iustifycacyōs/ that J be not confounded.

My soule hath faynted in thy health:and J haue trusted moche in thy worde.

Myne eyes haue faynted in thy promyse/sayēge when wylt thou conforte me.

For J am made lyke a bottell i the smoke:J ha= ue not forgoten thy commaundementes.

How many be the dayes of thy seruaunt/when thou wylt gyne iudgement of them that perse= cute me.

Wycked men haue shewed to me fables:but not as thy lawe.

All thy commaundementes is trueth:wycked men haue persecuted me/helpe me.

M iij

Almoſt they had conſumed in the earth:but I truly haue not foꝛſaken thy commaundementes

Quycken me accoꝛdynge to thy mercy/ꝛ I ſhall kepe the teſtymonies of thy mouthe.

O Loꝛde thy woꝛde doth remayne i heuyn euer laſtyngly.

Thy trueth frō generacyon to generacyon:thou haſt ſet the earth/and it ſhall abyde.

By thyne oꝛdinaunce the dayes cōtynue : foꝛ all thynges obey vnto the

Excepte thy lawe hadde ben my meditacyon: peraduenture I had peryſſhed in my humylite.

I ſhall neuer foꝛget thy iuſtifycacyons:foꝛ i thē thou haſt quyckened me.

I am thyne/make me ſafe:foꝛ I haue ſought out thy iuſtifycacyons.

Synners haue awayted me to deſtroye me/I haue vnderſtande thy teſtymonies.

I haue ſene the conſumacyon of euery ende:thy commaundemente is very large.

O Loꝛde how moche haue I loued thy lawe it is my meditacion all the day longe.

Thou haſt made me wyſe/ouer myn enemyes thꝛoughe thy cōmaundement foꝛ it is to me euer laſtynge.

I haue percepued moꝛe then all that taught me: foꝛ thy teſtymonies were my meditacyon.

I haue percepued moꝛe then auncyent men:by= cauſe I haue ſearched thy commaundementes.

I haue kepte my feete frō every eupll way : that I myght kepe thy woꝛdes.

I haue not declyned from thy iudgementes:foz
bycaule thou haſt ſet a lawe to me.

Howe ſwete be thy wozdes to my iawes:and to
my mouthe ſweter then hony.

I haue taken vnderſtādynge of thy cōmaūdemē
tes:therfoze haue J hated euery waye of iiquite.

Hy wozlde is a lāterne vnto my feete:and
a lyght vnto my patthes.

I haue ſwozne and decreed/tozkepe the iudge=
mentes of thy iuſtyce.

O lozde J am bzought lowe on euery ſyde:quyc=
ked me:accozdynge to thy wozde.

The voluntary thynges of my mouthe/o lozde
make them acceptable to the/and teache me thy
iudgementes.

My ſoule is euer in my handes:and J haue not
fozgoten thy lawe.

Sinners haue ſet a ſnare foz me:and J haue not
erred from thy commaundementes.

I haue goten thy teſtymonies by inheryptaunce
foz euer:fozbycauſe they be the iop of my herte.

Inclyne my hert to do thy iuſtifycacyōs foz euer:
foz rewarde.

I Haue hated the wycked : and haue loued
thy lawe.

Thou arte my helper and my defēder:and J ha=
ue truſted moche in thy wozde.

O ye wycked declyne ye frō me : and J ſhall ſer=
che the cōmaundementes of god.

Receyue me accozdynge to thy pzompſe : and
J ſhall lyue:noz thou ſhalte not confounde me

M iiij

other wyſe then I loked foz.

Helpe me & I ſhall be ſafe:and ſhal be ocupyed in thy iuſtyfycacyons euer.

Thou haſt deſpyſed al that go from thy iudge-mentes:foz theyz thoughtes were bniuſt.

I haue reputed all ſynners of the earthe foz offē-ders:therfoze I haue loued thy teſtymonyes.

I haue afflycted my fleſſhe foz feare of the:foz I am aferde of thy iudgementes.

I Haue done iuſtyce and ryghtwyſneſſe:thou ſhalte not delyuer me to them that caliip-niate me.

Receyue thy ſeruaūt ito goodnes:let not proude men calumpniate me.

Myne eyes haue fayled in thy healt:& the wozde of thy iuſtyce.

Do to thy ſeruaūt accozdynge to thy mercy and teache me thy iuſtyfycacyons.

I am thy ſeruaunt/gyue me bnderſtādynge that I may knowe thy teſtymonies.

It is tyme to do good lozde:foz they haue ſcatte-red abzode thy lawe.

Therfoze I haue loued thy commaundementes aboue golde and topaſe.

And therofoze I was let to all thy cōmaunde-mentes/I haue hated euery wycked way.

O Lozde meruaylous be thy teſtymonyes ther-foze my ſoule hath ſerched them.

The declaracyon of thy wozdes doth illumyne: and gyueth bnderſtandynge to the lytleons.

I haue opened my mouthe/and haue dzawē my

bzeath/foz bycanſe I deſyzed thy cōmaūdemētes

ⸯoke vpon me/and haue mercy vpon me/accoz
dynge to the iudgemēt of thē that loue thy name

ⸯyzect my goynges/accozdynge to thy wozde:⁊
let no iniquite reygne ouer me.

ⸯedeme me frō the calumniacyon of mē/that I
may kepe thy cōmaundementes.

ⸯllyghten thy face vpon thy ſeruaunt:and tea=
che me thy iuſtifycacyons.

ⸯyn eyes haue bzought fozth ſtreames of wa=
ter:bycauſe they haue not kepte thy lawe.

ⸯyghtuous arte thou lozd:and iuſte are thy
iudgementes.

ⸯhou haſt cōmaūded iuſtyce in thy teſtymonies:
and trueth mooſt chyefly.

ⸯhe loue of the cauſed me conſume:bycauſe my=
ne enemyes fozgat thy wozdes.

ⸯhy wozde is excedyngly fyzed:and thy ſeruaūt
loued it.

I am yonge and ſet at nought:yet haue I not
fozgoten thy cōmaundementes.

ⸯhy iuſtyce is euerlaſtynge:⁊ thy law is truth.

ⸯrouble and heuines haue intāgled me:thy cō=
maundementes are my ſtudye.

ⸯhy teſtymonies be gyuen in euerlaſtyng equi=
te:gyue me vnderſtandynge and I ſhall lyue.

ⸯaue called vpō the with all my herte:hea
re me lozde/foz I ſhal ſerch thy lawes.

ⸯ haue cryed vnto the/ſaue me:ſo that I may
obſerue thy cōmaundementes.

I haue pzeuented the tyme and haue cryed:foz

I haue greatly trusted in thy cōmaundementes.
Myn eyes haue preuented the daunyng of the
day:for to study thy worde.

Lorde heare my voyce / accordynge to thy mer=
cy:and quycken me accordynge to thy iudgemēt.

They that persecute me:haue encreased theyr
wyckednesse:but frō thy lawe they are:gon far=
re wyde.

Lorde thou art nere at hāde:and all thy wayes
are very trouth.

At the begynnynge I had knowledge of thy te=
stymonies:for thou hast establysshed thē for euer.

Beholde my humylite/and delyuer me:for
because I haue not forgoten thy lawe.

Iudge my iudgemēt/and redeme me:for thy pro
myse sake quyckest me.

Health is farre from synners:for they haue not
searched out thy iustyfycacyons.

Thy mercy lorde is moche:accordynge to thy
ryghtwysenes quycken me.

Many there be whiche persecute me and trouble
me:I haue not declyned from thy testymonies.

I sawe the offenders/and I was astonyed:for
they kepte not thy wordes.

Beholde lorde/for I haue loued thy cōmaunde=
mentes:quycken me in thy mercy.

The begynnyng of thy wordes is veryte:all thy
iudgementes are euerlastynge iustyce.

The prynces haue persecuted me:faut=
lesse:and my hert hath ben adrad of thy
wordes.

I shall be glad of thy wordes:as he that hath founde many spoyles.

I haue hated iniquite/and haue abhorred it:but thy lawe I haue loued.

Seuen tymes in a daye haue I praysed the:vpō the iudgementes of thy ryghtwysenes.

Great peace is to them that loue thy law:& there is no sclaunder in them.

I loked for thy saluacyon/o lorde:and I loued thy cōmaundementis.

My soule hath kepte thy testymonies:and hath loued them greatly.

I haue kepte thy cōmaundementes and thy testymonies:for all my wayes are in thy syght.

Lorde let my prayer approche nere in thy syght:gyue me vnderstandynge:accordyng to thy promyse.

O lorde let my prayer entre in to thy syght:delyuer me/accordynge to thy promyse.

My lyppes shal powre forth thy prayse:when thou hast taught me thy iustyfycacyons.

My tongue shall shewe forth thy promyse : for in all thy cōmaundementes is equite.

Let thy hande be redy to helpe me:for bycause I haue chosen thy cōmaundementes.

O lorde I haue desyred thy helth:and thy lawe is my medytacyon.

My soule shall lyue/and shall prayse the:& thy iudgementes shall helpe me.

I haue wandered lyke a shepe/whiche is losse/o lorde seke out thy seruaunt/for I haue not for getten thy cõmaundementes.

Loꝛde gyue them eternall reste: ⁊ let contynuall lyght shyne vnto them.

Loꝛde haue mercy on vs. Chꝛyste haue mercy on vs. Loꝛde haue mercy on vs. Our father whiche arte in heuyn. Hayle Mary full of grace.

LOꝛde thou hast pꝛoued me/and knowẽ me: thou haste knowen my downe syttynge ⁊ vpꝛysynge.

Thou haste perceyued my thoughtes a farre of: my patthe and the strynge of my lyfe thou hast searched out.

And all my wayes thou haste pꝛcuasted: so that there is not one woꝛde on my tongue.

Lo loꝛde thou hast knowen all thynges bothe newe and olde: thou hast fourmed me /⁊ put thy hande vpon me.

The connyng that thou hast wꝛought on me is merueylous: it is wꝛought so that I cã not attayne in to it.

Whyter shal I go frõ thy spyꝛyt: and whyther shall I flye from thy face.

If I shal ascende vp to heuyn/thou arte there ⁊ yf I shal descende downe in to hel: thou art also pꝛesent.

If I shall take my wynges in the moꝛnyng: and shall dwell in the farthest coostes of the see.

Yet shall thy hãde bꝛynge me frõ thens: and thy ryght hande shall holde me.

And I haue sayd peraduẽture the darknes shal treade me vnder feete: ⁊ the nyght is my lyght in thy delytes.

For the darkenes shall not be hyd frō the / and the nyght shall be as lyght as the day: for as his lyght is / so is his darkenes.

For thou hast possessed my raynes: thou hast taken me from the wombe or my mother.

I shall confesse to the / that thou arte terryble & meruaylous: thy workes be wonderous / and my soule knoweth it to well.

My bones is not hydde frō the / which thou hast made preuyly: my substaūce within the in warde partes of the earth.

Thyne eyes haue sene myne imperfectenes: and in thy boke are wryten: all dayes they were fourmed and no man was in them.

O god thy frendes ar greatly honoured of me & the chepf of them is ouer moche strengthed.

I shall nombre thē / and they shall be multiplyed aboue the grauell: I haue rysen vp / and yet am with the.

O god yf thou woldest slee the synners: ye bloudy men go ye away from me.

For ye say in your thought: they take in vayne theyr cytyes.

Do not I hate them (good lorde) that hate the & was I not angry with thyne enemyes.

I haue hated them with a feruēt hate: and they be myne enymyes.

Proue me good lorde and knowe my herte questyon with me / and knowe my wayes.

And loke yf the way of iniquite be in me / and

bꝛynge me in to the way euerlastynge.
The verse. Loꝛde gyue them eternall reste.
The answere. And let eternal lyght shyne vnto
the. The verse. Frō the gates of hell. The answe.
Loꝛde delyuer theyr soules. The verse. I truste to
se the goodes of the loꝛde. The answere. In the
lande of the lyuynge. The verse. Loꝛde heare my
pꝛayer. The answere. And let my cꝛyenge come
vnto the. The answere.

O the loꝛde we cōmende the soules of thy
seruauntes / bothe men and women: so that
they that be deade to the woꝛlde may lyue to the
and all the synnes that they haue committed by
fraylte of woꝛldely couersacyon: thou loꝛde wasshe them away / by the foꝛgyuenes of thy moost
mercyfull pyte. By Chꝛyst our loꝛde.
God haue mercy on al chꝛysten soules. So be it.

The prayer of the pꝛophet Ionas delyuered out of the whales bely.

IN my afflyccyon I cryed vn
to the loꝛde: & he answered
me. Euyn frō the bellye of hell I
cryed / and thou hardest my voyce /
foꝛ thou hadst thꝛowen me foꝛth
in the myddes of the depest of the
see / and the waters closed me rounde aboute all thy greatwaters
and flodes wente ouer me / & I thought / sayenge
with my selfe / I am cast out of thy syght / I shall
neuer moꝛe se thy holy tēple: foꝛ waters haue cōpassed euyn vppe to my soule. The darke depth

closed me in/and the foule stynkynge wedes of
the see couered my heade. I sanke downe vn=
der the hylles so that the waters barred me out
from the earth for euer:and thou dyddest pteser=
ue my lyfe from destruccyon (oh lozde my god)
when my soule fayled me/yet I remembzed the
lozde/and my ptayer came vnto thy holy temple.
They that are gyuen to vanites and lyes/haue
lost theyz mercy from god/but I shal offre vnto
the lozde ptayse/and shall perfourme my vowes
to the lozde/whiche is a sauyoure.

The argument of the Psalmes of the Passyon.

FOz asmoch as in these psalmes folowyng
dyuerse ptophecyes cōcernyng the passyō/
death and resurreccyon of our sauyoure Chzyste
are conteyned/therfoze are they called Psalmes
of the passyō:wherin Dauid exptessyng/& beyng
the fygure of Chzyste/doth fyzst/as it were in a
songe/recozde and exptesse his great wreccyon &
downefal/& after that his sodeyn exaltacyon and
rysyng agayne/the cōfucyon of his aduersaries
the restozyng of his kyngdome with the encrease
and dilatynge of the same/euyn to the vttermost
parte of the earth/and fynally the contynuaunce
therof vnto the wozldes ende. And euyn so dyd
our medyatour Chzyst/fyzst suffre the death of
the crosse/whiche to the face of the wozlde was
rpght shameful and sclaunderous / and after
that rose agayne with hygh glozy and trymphe/

The argumēt of the Psalmes of þ Psallyō.
when he hadde obteyned vyctory agaynst the de=
uyll/death/and synnc/ꝛ delyuer his kyngedome
(whiche is the Churche)from the strayghte obly=
gacyon and bonde of death in the whiche it was
wrapped by the offence of Adā/and destroyed the
Churche Malygnant/the kyngdome and Syna=
goge of Sathan with the myghty spiryte of his
mouthe/J meane the vertue of his euerlastynge
worde/wherby he shall preserue and contynue
his sayde kyngdome oꝛ Churche vnto þ worldes
ende. Whiche as he dyd at the begynnynge by
his apostles/so shal he by his true preachers di=
late and extēde the same in to all the costes of the
worlde/and at the latter resurreccyon/shall dely
uer it vp vnto his father/pure and vnspotted/to
be immoꝛtally gloꝛyfyed in body and soule:euyn
as verily as he hym selfe arose agayn frō death/
and ascended vnto his father in body and soule
eternally to reygne with hym in heuyn.

The Psalmes of the Psalter.

Deus deus meus respice.

The .xxii. Psalme.

 God my god:loke towarde me/why
hast thou forsaken me:far from my
health be the wordes of my synnes
My god/J wyll crye & call to the
by daye/& thou wylt not hear me:&
euyn so by nyght/& thou wylt not
impute to myn ygnoraunce.

Thou truely dwellest i the hooly place:the pray=
se of Israel.

Our fathers haue trusted in the/they haue tru=
R j

ted/and thou haste delyuered them.

They haue cryed to the/and they be made safe
they haue trusted in the/and they were not con=
founded.

I truly am but a worme/and no man: the appro
bry of men/and out cast of all the people.

All that euer sawe me laughed me to skorne:
they spake with theyr lyppes / and noded with
theyr heades.

Sayenge he hath trusted in the lorde: nowe let
hym take hym/let hym make hym hole/for he
loueth hym.

For thou arte he that haste drawen me from
the wombe/and wast myne hope from the brestes
of my mother: I was cast out from my mothers
wombe vnto the.

Thou arte my god from my mothers wombe de=
parte not from me.

For tribulacyon is nere: and there is none to
helpe me.

Many calues haue compassed me: and fatte bul=
les haue beset me aboute.

They haue set theyr mouthes wyde open vpon
me: lyke a lyon raumpynge and rorynge.

I was powred forth lyke water: and all my bo=
nes were dispersed a sonder.

My herte was made lyke meltyng waxe/with in
the myddes of my belly.

My strength was dryed vp lyke a shelle: my ton=
gue cleaued fast to my iawes: & thou hast brought
me to deade dustle.

For dogges compasse me aboute:the counsell of euyll men haue beset me.

They haue bored my handes and my feete:they haue nombred all my bones.

They truely haue consydered and loke vpõ me: and haue deuyded amonge them my garmentes: and vpon my cote they haue cast lottes.

Prolonge not good lorde thy helpe from me:but loke vnto my defence.

Delyuer my soule frõ the swerde:and myne one= ly soule from the hande of the dogge.

Saue me from the mouth of the lyon:and my hu= mylite from the hornes of vnycornes.

I shal shewe thy name to my brethren & I shal prayse the in the myddes of the congregacyon.

Ye that feare the lorde prayse ye hym:all the ho= le seede of Jacob gloryfye ye hym.

Let all the sede of Israel feare hym:for he despy= seth not/nor tourneth his face from the prayer of the poore.

Neyther turneth he awaye his face frõ me : and when I cryed vnto hym he hath herde me.

At the shall my prayse be in the great congrega= cyon:I shal yelde vp my vowes in the syght of them that feare hym.

Let poore men eate/and they shall be satis= fyed/and they shall prayse the lorde : that seke after hym: theyr hertes mouthe lyue worlde with ende.

All the costes of the earth shall remembre them selues/and shall be conuerted to the lorde.

K ij

nd all the familyes of the gentylles shall do worshyp in his presence.

or to the lorde apperteyneth kyngdome and he shall rule the people.

ll the ryche men of the earth haue eaten and worshypped hym: al that shal descende in to the earth/shall bowe downe in his syght.

nd my soule shall lyue to hym: & my seede shall serue hym.

he generacyon to come shal be shewed to the lorde: and the heuyns shal shew the iustyce that he hath done to the people that shall be borne.

Ominus regit me. The lorde ruleth me. &c Ye shall fynde in the Dirige.

Omini est terra. &c. The eart his the lordes his Psalme is in the Matyns.

D te domie leuaui. nto the lorde haue. &c his psalme is in the Dirige.

Iudica me domine. The .rrb. psalme

Udge me good lorde / for I haue entred in myn innocencye: and trustynge in the lorde/ I shall not be made weyke.

roue me good lorde and tempte me/bothe my raynes and my herte.

or thy mercy is before myne eyes : and I haue delyted in thy trouth.

haue not sytten with a vayne counsell neyther shall I medle with them that do vniustly.

haue hated the congregacyon of the malygnāt: and with the vngodly I shal not sytte.

shall wasshe my handes amonge the innocen:

tes:& I shal compasse aboute thy aultare/o lorde
that I may hear the voyce of thy laud and that
I may shewe forth all thy wonderous workes.

Lorde I haue loued the beautye of thy house:&
the dwellynge place of thy glory.

O god destroy not my soule with the wycked:nor
my lyfe with bloudsheders.

In whose handes is wyckednesse:& theyr ryght
hande is fylled with brybes.

I truely haue entred in myne innocēcye/redemē
me/and haue mercy vpon me.

My god hath stande ryght vp/o lorde:in the con
gregacyons I shall prayse the.

Domin9 illuminatio mea. The lorde is my
lyght. Ye shal fynde it in the Dirige.

Ad te domine clamabo.

Lorde I shall cry to the /o god my god/be
not longe sylent towarde me/leste ẏ when
thou shalt holde thy peace to me/I shall be lyke=
ned to them that descende downe in to the lake.

O good lorde heare ẏ voyce of my prayer/whyle
I pray to the:whyle I lyfte vp my handes vnto
thy holy temple.

That thou delyuer me not amonge the synners
& that thou do not loose me amonge theym that
worke iniquite.

Whiche speake peace to theyr neyghbour:and
theyr hertes be full of euyll.

Gyue vnto thē accordynge to theyr workes and
accordynge to the wyckednes of theyr inuēcyōs
rewarde them.

R iij

gyue vnto them accordynge to the workes of
theyr handes so gyue them theyr rewarde.

For because they haue not vnderstāde the wor=
kes of the lorde/and in the workes of theyr han=
de/thou shalte destroy them/and thou shalt not
edifye them.

The lorde is blessed for he hath herd the voyce
of my complaynt.

The lord is my helper and my defender:& in hym
hath my herte trusted/and I haue ben holpen.

And my flesshe hath restoryffhed:and I shall be
confessed to hym with al my wyll.

The lorde is the strength of his people:and he
is the defender of the helth of his anoynted.

O good lorde make safe thy people:& blesse thy=
ne herytaūce:and gouerne them and extolle thē
for euer.

Afferte domino filij.

Brynge to the lord/o ye sones of god/bryng
to the lorde the sones of rammes.

Brynge ye to the lorde glory and honour:bryng
ye to the lorde the glory of his name: prayse ye
the lorde in his holy courte.

The voyce of the lorde/vpō the waters:the god
of maiestye hath thondered/the lorde ouer many
waters.

The voyce of the lorde i vertue:the voyce of the
lorde in excellencye.

The voyce of the lorde breakynge þ Cedre trees
and the lord shal breake euyn the Cedre trees of
Lybany.

And he shall destroy them lyke a calfe of lybany
and he is loued lyke as the sones of vnicornes.

The voyce of the lorde cuttyng the flãbes of fyre
the voyce of the lorde beatynge the desarte & the
lorde shall meue the deserte Cades.

The voyce of the lorde preparyng hertes:and he
shal open the thycke places: and i his temple all
men shall gyue glory.

The lorde maketh the great flonde to inhabyt:
and he shall reygne kynge for euer.

The lorde shall gyue vertue vnto his people:the
lorde shall blesse his people in peace.

Exaltabo te domine qm.

I Shall exalte the(O lorde)for thou haste de
fended me:neyther hast thou suffered myn
enemyes to haue theyr pleasure vpon me.

O lorde my god/I haue cryed vnto the: & thou
hast healed me.

Lorde thou hast brought my soule out of the
lowe place:thou hast preserued me from thẽ that
descende in to the pytte.

Synge vnto the lorde ye that be his sayntes: &
confesse ye the memory of his holynes.

For there is vengeãce in his displeasure: and
lyfe in his pleasure.

At the euenynge mournynge shall contynue:&
in the mornynge gladnesse.

Verily I sayd in my welthynesse: I shall neuer
more be moued.

Lorde through thy good wyll thou hast lente
strength vnto my beauty.

Thou turnest thy face from me:and I was al astonyed.

Unto the lorde shall I crye:& shall make prayer vnto my god.

What profyte is there in my bloude/whē I shall descende in to corrupcyon.

Shall dust make knowledge vnto the:or shal it publysshe thy trouth.

The lorde hath herde/& hath had mercy on me: and the lorde is made myne helper.

Thou hast tourned my sorowe i to ioye:thou haste cutte my sacke/and haste compassed me with gladnesse.

To the ende that my glory myght syng to the and myght not be prycke:o my lorde god/I shall euermore confesse the.

In te domine speraui.   The .rrr. Psalme

IN the lorde haue I trusted/let me not be confounded for euer/delyuer me i thy rygh- tuousnesse.

Inclyne thyne eare vnto me:make haste to de- lyuer me.

Be thou to me a god:and a protectour:& a place of refuge/that thou mayst make me safe.

For thou art my strength and my refuge : & for thy names sake thou shalte conduyte me/& shalte norysshe me.

Thou shalt brynge me out of the snare : whiche they haue layde preuylye for me:for thou arte my protectoure.

In to thy handes/o lorde/do I commende my spi-

rite:o lorde god of trueth thou hast redemed me.
Chryst was made obedient for vs
vnto death/euyn vnto the death of the crosse.
Holy mother of god pray to thy sone.
That we may be enabled to his
promyssyon. Greatly to be praysed is
Johan the Euangelyst. Whiche
leaned on the brest of Jesu Chryste.

Egarde we beseche the lord/this thy hous=
holde/for the whiche our lorde Jesu chryst
hath not doubted to be delyuered to the handes
of euyll doers/& to suffre the payne of the crosse.
Lorde Jesu chryst I beseche the of thy goodnes
to accepte the intercessid of the glorious virgyn
Mary/thy moost holy mother/for vs bothe nowe
and at the houre of death/whose moost blessed
herte the swerde of sorowe dydde pearce at the
houre of thy passyon.
Lorde god we beseche the/that the prayer of
blessed saynt Johan thy apostle and Euange=
lyst may be euer auaylable to vs bothe nowe and
at the houre of death:to whom when thou wast
dyeng on the crosse/dydest commende the virgyn
thy mother.Whiche lyuest and reygnest/O god
worlde withdut ende.So be it.
The gloryous passyon of our lorde Jesu Chryst
delyuer vs from sorowfull heuynesse:and bryng
vs to the ioyes of paradyse.So be it.
To the holy and indiuisible Trinyte/to the hu=
manyte of Jesu Chryst crucifyed/and to the glo=
ryous virgyn Mary/glory infinite be gyuen of

Saynt hieroms psalter.
euery creature worlde withthout ende. So be it.

A haple moost benygne Iesu /full of mercy
and grace. Blessed be thy passyon death ꝧ
woundes/and blyssed be the bloude of thy body.
Lord haue mercy on me wretched synner. Moost
swete lord gyue vnto me a cleane ꝧ a cōtryte herte quiete/ꝧ pacient:a bodye chaste / humble/obe-
dient/and stable/and alwaye redy to thy seruyce
Which lyuest and reygnest god/worlde without
ende. So be it.

The argument of saynt Hieroms Psalter.

BEcause it is vnknowen who fyrst gathered
all the verses togyther that we call saynt
Hieroms Psalter/therfore of the begynnynge ꝧ
purpose of the seruyce/I can declare nothynge
for certayne:for though it go forth vnder the name of saynt hierom:yet is it vncertayne whether
euer he were author therof or not/seynge it doth
not so appere by any of his workes:nor by any
other approued history but only i a rubryke that
is sette before it in latyn/which maketh mēcyon
that the angel of god shulde teache it hym/with
suche other prety persuasions. But who soeuer
were the maker therof/true it is/that ꝧ redynge
therof is not vnfruytfull.

The Psalter of saynt Hierome.

Verba mea auribus percipe domine.

LOrde perceyue my wordes with thyne eares vnderstande thou my complaynt.
O my kynge/my god/intende to the voyce of my
prayer.

O good lorde reproue me not in thyne ire:nor in thy fury do not chastyce me.

Haue mercy on me good lorde/for I am sycke: hele me good lorde:for al my bones ar troubled.

And my soule is greatly troubled:but o lorde how longe.

Tourne the good lorde & delyuer my soule:make me saue for thy mercy.

Loke vpon me and heare me/o lorde my god.

Illumyne myne eyes that I slepe not in death.

Perfourme my goinges in thy patthes:that my steppes may not be remoued.

I haue cryed out for thou hast hard me:o god in clyne thyne eare to me/and heare my wordes.

Make thy mercy meruaylous:thou which sauest them that truste in the.

Kepe me good lorde lyke the balle of thyne iye defende me vnder the shadow of thy wynges:frō the face of the wycked whiche haue troubled me

Clense me good lorde from my secretes:and frō straunge thynges spare thy seruaunt.

But thou good lorde let not thy helpe be farre from me:loke vnto my defence.

O god delyuer my soule frō the swerde : and my only soule from the hande of the dogge.

Saue me frō the mouthe of the lyon:and my humylyte from the hornes of vnycornes.

I shall shewe thy name to my brethrene in the myddes of the congregacyon I shal prayse the.

O lorde make thy wayes knowen vnto me : and teache me the pathes/& direct me in thy trueth.

Haue mynde good lorde of thy mercyes:and of thy mercyfulnes whiche haue ben frō the begyn=nyng of the worlde.

The offences of my youth/and myn ygnoraun=ces do not remembre good lorde.

Accordynge to thy mercy haue remembraunce of me:for thy trueth good lorde.

For thy names sake thou shalt take pyte of my synne:for why it is great.

Beholde my humylyte and my labour:and for=gyue all myne offences.

Destroy not my soule (o god) with the wycked: nor my lyfe with the bloudsheders.

Lorde heare my voyce/with the whiche I haue cryed to the:haue mercy on me and heare me.

Turne not thy face from me:nor i thy wrath do not swarue from thy seruaunt.

Good lord be thou my helper/do not forsake me nor despyce me:o god/my healt.

O good lorde set me a law in thy way:and direct me in thy ryght path/for feare of my enemyes.

Delyuer me not at the pleasure of thē that trou ble me:for they haue rysen agaynst me.

To the/o lorde I crye/o my god/be not sylent to= warde me:nor do ꝑ not at anye tyme go awaye from me:for then I shalbe lyke to them that de= scende in to the lake.

O good lorde heare the voyce of my prayer/why le I praye to the/whyle I lyft vp my handes to thy holy temple.

Delyuer not me amonge the synners:nor w not

destroye me with them that worke iniquite.

O lorde make safe thy people and blysse then inherytaunce.

And gouerne them and extoll them for euer.

In the lorde haue I trusted/let me neuer be confounded:in the ryghtuousnes delyuer me.

Incline to me thy ere:make hast to delyuer me.

Be thou to me a god/a defender:and in the house of refuge:that thou mayst make me safe.

In to thy handes (good lorde) do I commende my spyryte.

Delyuer me and take me frō the hādes of myne enemyes.

Enlyghten thy face vpon thy seruaūt:make me safe in thy mercy good lorde/let me not be confounded/for bycause I haue trusted in the.

Let thy mercy lorde be done vpon vs:lyke as we haue trusted in the.

I shal blesse the lorde in euery tyme: his prayse shall be euer in my mouthe.

My soule shal be praysed in the lorde:the meke shall heare/and they shal be glad.

Magnifye ye the lord with me/and let vs exalte his name in to it selfe.

O lorde iudge thē that hurte me/and ouercome them that be agaynst me.

Take vp weapons and a shelde/and ryse vnto my helpe.

Be not sylent/o lorde/nor do not departe from me/and aryse and intende in to my iudgement/ my god and my lorde intende to my cause.

Iudge me good lorde/and my god/accordynge to my ryghtuousnes.

Stretche forth good lorde/thy mercy to the that knowe the:and thy ryghtuousnes to the whiche be of good mynde.

Let not the foote of pryde come to me:nor let not the hande of a synner moue me.

Heare myn oracyon good lorde and my prayer recepue them in thyn eares/whyles I wepe.

Be not sylent/bycause I am but a straūger with the and a pilgrym:lyke as al my forefathers.

Spare me that I myght breath a lytel before I go:and shall neuer be here more.

But thou good lorde/let not thy helpe be longe from me:thy mercy and thy trueth haue euer defended me.

For so many myscheues haue cōpassed me that they can not be nōbred:myn iniquites haue comprehended me/and I had no power to se them.

They haue ben multiplied more thē the heeres of my head:and my herte hath forsaken me.

May it please the good lorde to delyuer me:good lorde loke to my helpe.

For truely I am nedy and poore:good lord take cure of me.

Thou arte my helper and my defeder(o my god) be not slowe.

I haue sayd(o lorde)haue mercy vpon me:heale my soule/for I haue synned agaynst the.

Ryse vp lorde why doest thou slombre; aryse & do not repelle me to the ende.

Why turnest thou away thy face/and forgettest
our nedynes/and our tribulacyons.

Aryse vp lorde helpevs: and delyuer vs for thy
names sake.

Haue mercy on me o god: accordyng to thy great
mercy.

And accordyng to the multitude of thy mercyes
put away my wyck dnes.

And wasshe me cl ane frõ myne vniustyce: and
clẽse me from my faultes.

For I do knowe myne iniquite: and my synne is
euer agaynst me.

I haue synned to the alonly/ & I haue done euyll
before the/that thou myghtest be iustyfyed in all
thy wordes: and that thou mayst ouercome when
thou shalte be iudged.

Lo surely I am cõceyued in iniquite: and my mo
ther hath conceyued me in synnes.

Lo truely thou hast loued trueth: the vncertay
ne and the secrete thynges of thy wysdome thou
hast magnifyed to me.

Thou shalte sprynkle me good lorde with hyso
pe/and I shal be made cleane: thou shalt wasshe
me/and I shall be made whyther then snowe.

To my hearyng thou shalte gyue ioye & gladnes
and the humbled bones shall sprynge for ioye.

Tourne thy face awaye from my synnes and put
away all myne iniquite.

O god create i me a cleane herte: & renue a ryght
spirite in my bowelles.

Put me not away from thy face: nor take not

away thy holy spirite from me.

Gyue vnto me the gladnes of thy health/and cō
fyrme me with thy pryncypall spirite.

O lorde thou shalte opē my lyppes/& my mouthe
shall shewe thy prayse.

O god make me safe in thy name/and in thy ver
tue iudge me.

O god heare my prayer/and with thyne eares re
ceyue the wordes of my mouth.

For straungers haue rysen agaynst me/& strōge
men haue sought my soule/& they haue set god
before theyr syght.

O god heare my requeste/and do not despyse my
prayer/intende to me and heare me.

In god I prayse the worde/in the lorde I shal
prayse the speche/I haue trusted in god/I shal
not feare any thynge that man can do to me.

O god i me ben the vowes/whiche I shall yelde
vnto the prayse of the.

For thou hast delyuered my soule frō death my
feete frō fallynge/that I may please before god
in the lande of the lyuynge.

Haue mercy on me good lord/haue mercy on me
for my soule trusteth in the.

And I shall truste i the shadowe of thy wynges/
vntyll iniquite ouerpasse.

Take me from them that worke iiquite/and sa=
ue me from bloudsheders.

For lo they haue taken my soule/the stronge ha
ue fallen vpon me.

I truely haue made my prayer to the/o god/in

tyme acceptable.

In the multitude of thy mercyes heare me: i the beryte of thy health.

Helpe me out of the claye/that I stycke not fast/ delyuer me from them that hate me:and frō the depnes of waters.

Let not the tēpest of water drowne me : nor let not the depnes swalowe me vp : nor let not the pyt open his mouthe vpon me.

Heare me good lorde / for thy mercy is bounte= ous:loke vpon me /accordynge to the multitude of thy mercyes.

Intende to my soule & delyuer it/take me away for feare of myne enemyes.

O god intende to my helth : lorde make hast to helpe me.

For I truly am nedy & poore/o god helpe me.

O lorde be thou my helper and my delyuerer: do not tary.

In the o lorde haue I trusted/let me not be con= founded for euer:i thy ryghtuousnes delyuer me.

Inclyne thyne eare to me/and heale me.

Be thou to me a god and a defender:and in stede of a bulwerke that thou mayst make me safe.

My god delyuer me from the handes of a synner: and from the handes of a wycked mā/that wor= keth agaynst the lawe.

Let my mouthe be fulfylled with prayse:that I may synge thy glory all the daye longe / and thy magnifycence.

Cast me not away in the tyme of my age : when

S

my ftrength fhall fayle me fozfake not me.

god kepe not thy felfe afarre from me : o my god / loke to my helpe.

truely fhall hope in the : and J fhall euer adde aboue all thy laude.

Delyuer not to beftes the foules of the that con felle the : and the foules of thy pooze men do not fozget at length.

Loke vpon thy teftament / foz they be fulfylled whiche haue endarked the earth / with the hou: fes of iniquite.

Helpe vs o god our fauyour : and foz the glozy of thy name o lozde delyuer vs / and be mercyfull to our fynnes / foz thy names fake.

Eyfe vp thy power and come : that thou mayfte make vs faufe.

O lozde god of vertues conuert vs / and fhew thy face / and we fhall be faufe.

Conuerte vs / o god our fauyour / & turne away thy wzathe from vs.

Wylt thou be wzath with vs foz euer / oz wylt thou ertende thyne ire frõ generacyõ and pgeny.

O god thou beynge turned fhalt quyckẽ vs : and thy people fhall ioye in the.

O lozde fhewe vs thy mercy : and gyue vs thy health.

O lozde felyne thyn eare / and heare me foz J am nedy and pooze.

Kepe my foule / foz J am a fynner / o my god ma: ke hole thy feruaunt / that trufteth in the.

Haue mercy on me good lozd : foz J haue cryed

to y all y day:englade y soule of thy seruaūt/for
bycause/o lorde I haue lyfted vp my soule vnto
the. Ānd thou lorde god arte a minyster of mer=
cy/and arte mercyfull:pytifull / pacyent / and of
moche mercy/and also true.

Loke vpō me/and haue mercy ou me:gyue thy=
ne Ēmpere to thy chylde:and make safe the ser=
uaunt of thyne hande mayde.

Make me a sygne in goodnes/ that they that ha
ue hated me may se me/& be cōfounded: for thou
good lorde haste holpē me/and hast cōforted me.

O lorde god of my health/I haue cryed to the in
the daye/and in the nyght before the.

Let my prayer entre in to thy syght:inclyne thy
ne eare vnto my prayer.

O lorde where be thyne olde mercyes: lyke as y
hast sworne to Dauyd in the trueth.

O lorde haue in mynde the obbrobry of thy ser=
uaunt/whiche I haue conteyned in my bosom of
many people.

Turne agayne lorde yet hytherto:and vouchsa=
fe that thy seruaunt myght pray to the.

And let the glory of the lorde our god be vpon
vs/& vpon the workes of our handes directe vs/
and directe the workes of our handes.

O lorde heare my prayer: and let my crye come
vnto the.

Tourne not away thy face from me: in what
daye soeuer I am troubled: inclyne thyne eare
vnto me.

In what daye soeuer I shall calle vpō the: here

S ij

me with spede.

And leade me not forth in the myddest of my dayes/from generacyon in to the generacyon of thy peare.

And thou lorde do good vnto me for thy names sake/for thy mercy is swete.

O lorde delyuer me/for I am nedy and poore: & my herte is troubled within me.

I am banysshed away lyke a shadow/when it declyneth:& I am crushed togyther lyke a locust.

Helpe me o god my god/and saue me for thy mercye.

Rewarde thy seruaunt/quycken me:and obser= ue thy wordes.

Open myne eyes/and I shal consydre the mer= uayles of thy lawe.

I am but a straunger in the earth:hyde not thy commaundementes from me.

My soule hath alwayes desyred to knowe thy ryghtuousnes.

Thou hast blamed the proude:they be cursed that declyne from thy commaundementes.

Take away from me rebuke and contempte:for I haue sought after thy lawes.

For prynces haue sytte & spoken agaynst me.

The way of iniquite remoue from me: and of thy lawe haue mercy on me.

I haue chosen the way of trouth:I haue not for gotten thy iudgementes.

Leade me in to the patthe of thy commaunde= mentes:for that is that I wolde.

Inclyne myne herte in to thy lawes/ and not to couetyſe.

Turne awaye myne eyes that they ſe not vany: te:and quycken me in thy way.

Make ſure thy ſeruaunt in thy worde:in the ſca re of the.

Teache me goodnes lernynge/and ſcyence:for I haue beleued thy commaundementes.

Thou arte good/and in thy goodnes teache me thy iuſtyfycacyons.

Let thy mercye be that it may exorte me / accor dynge to thy promyſe to thy ſeruaunt.

Let thy mercyes come to me: & I ſhal lyue /for thy lawe is my meditacyon.

Let my herte be imaculate in thy iuſtyfycacyōs/ that I be not confounded.

O lorde I am brought lowe on al partes quyc: ken me accordynge to thy worde.

O lorde lette the volūtarye thynges of thy mou the be acceptable vnto the:& teache me thy iud: gementes.

My ſoule is euer in my handes:and I haue not forgotten thy lawe.

Take me accordynge to thy promyſe / & I ſhall lyue:and thou ſhalte not confounde me / other: wyſe then I loked for.

Helpe me/and I ſhall be ſafe/and I ſhall be oc cupped in thy meditacyons.

Do to thy ſeruaunt accordynge to the mercy: & teache me thy iuſtyfycacyons.

I am thy ſeruaunt/ gyue me vnderſtandynge:

S iij

that I may knowe thy wyll.

Loke vpon me & haue mercy vpō me/accordyng
to the iudgementes of them that loue thy name.

Dyrecte my steppes accordynge to thy promyse:
and no iniquite shall ouercome me.

Dlysse me from the iniuryes of mē: that I may
kepe my commaundementes.

Lyghten thy face vpon thy seruaunt: teache me
thy iustyfycacyons.

Beholde my humilyte/and delyuer me: for I ha=
ue not forgotten thy lawe.

Iudge my iudgement and redeme me / quycken
me for thy promyse.

O lorde lette my prayer approche nere in thy
syght: delyucr me accordynge to thy promyse.

Let my prayer entre in to thy syght: delyuer me
accordynge to thy promyse.

My lyppes shal powre forth thy prayse / when ȳ
hast taught me thy iustyfycacyons.

My tongue shall shewe forth thy worde for I all
thy commaundementes is equite.

Let thy hāde be redy to helpe me: forbycause I
haue chosyn thy commaundementes.

O lorde I haue desyred thy healthe: & thy lawe
is my meditacyon.

My soule shall lyue and shall prayse the: and thy
iudgementes shall helpe me.

I haue wandered lyke a slepe/that was losse: o
lorde seke out thy seruaunt/for I haue not for=
gotten thy commaundementes.

Haue mercy on me lorde/haue mercy on me/for

we be replete full of contempte.

Good lorde do well to thē that be good / and of ryght mynde.

O lorde turne away our captyuyte / as a ryuer in the southe wynde.

I haue cryed to the from the hyest places; o lorde hear my prayer.

Let thyne eares be entendynge to the voyce of my prayer.

In what day soeuer J shall call vpō the / heare ÿ me / thou shalte encrease strengthe in my soule.

O lorde set a keper ouer my mouth / and a dore ouer my lyppes.

Declyne not myne herte in to wordes of maly= ce / to make excuses in synne.

Intende to my prayer: for J am humbled very moche.

Delyuer me from thē that psecute me: for they haue preuayled agaynst me.

Brynge my soule forth of pryson / that it may cō fesse thy name.

O lorde heare my prayer / receyue my request in to thyn eares / heare me in thy ryghtuousnes.

And thou shalte not entre with thy seruaūt in Iudgement / for there is none lyuynge / that cā be iustifyed in the syght of the.

For myne enemye hath psecuted my soule: and hath humbled my lyfe in the earth.

He hath set me in darkenes lyke the dead men of the worlde: ⁊ my soule is greued within me / in me my herte is troubled.

I haue i mīde myne olde dayes/ I haue thought
vpon al thy workes: and vpon al the workes of
thy handes I mused.

I haue caste myne hādes abrode to the (o my sou
le) lyke the earth without water.

Heare me quyckly good lorde / for my spyrite
fayleth.

Thou shalt not tourne away thy face from me: ī
I shal be lyke them that go downe in to a lake.

Let thy mercy be knowen to me: betyme for I
haue trusted in the.

Let me knowe the waye / in whiche I shall
walke: for I haue lyfte vp my soule to the.

Delyuer me lorde from myn enemyes: I haue
fled to the: teache me to do thy wyll / for thou
arte my god.

Thy good spyryte shall brynge me in to the
ryght lande: for thy name thou shalte quycken
me in thy ryghtuousnes.

Thou shalte brynge my soule out of tribulacy:
on: and in thy mercy thou shalte destroye all my
ne enemyes.

And thou shalt destroy all that trouble my sou
le: for I am thy seruaunt. ¶ The prayer.

Grante I beseche the lorde god/ that by the
holy melody of this heuynly psalter/ my sou
le may be refresshed. Graūt that the roryng lyō
may be ouercom of the feble shepe. Graunt that
by thy grace/ the moost violēt spirite may be sub
dued of the weyke flesshe. Graūt that he/ whiche
fell from heuyn may be vāquysshed here through

my fyghtynge. Graunt that thoughe we abyde
his tyranny / through thy sufferaūce for a season /
that yet we be not swalowed vp with his vnsa-
cyable iawes. Cause hym to be sory for mannes
saluacyon / whiche alwayes reioyseth at our fall.
Cause me alwayes to applye my selfe to thy
praysynge / and at length ioyfully to come to thy
blyssednes / whiche lyuest and reygnest god worlde without ende. So be it.

¶A prayer to saynt Hierom.
Amator humani.

O God the louer of mankynde / whiche by thyne electe seruaunt and bysshop saynt hierō
hast renewed in the worlde the gyft of tongues:
wherwith in tyme passed thou dydest heuynly instructe thyne apostles / for the preachynge of thy
gospel by thym holy spirite: graūt that in all tongues / and i all places / all mē may preache the glory of thyne onely begotten sōne Iesu / for to confounde the tonges of false apostles / whiche con-
spyrynge togyther / do buyld the cursed toure of
Babylō / laboryng to darken thy glorye whylest
they procure to exalte theyr owne / where as all
glory is due onely to ye with our
lorde Iesu thy sone worlde without ende. So be it.

¶Whē thou shalte receyue the
sacrement. Dne non sum dignus
vt intres sub tectum.

O Mercyfull lorde / I am not
worthy that ye shuldest en-

tre in to my synfull house yet not withstandynge
thou hast sayd; who that eateth my flesshe & dzyn
keth my bloude/he dwelleth i me/ and J in hym.
Wherfoze lozde haue thou mercy vp me synner/
by the recepyyng of this thy body/flesshe & blou=
de. And that J recepue it not to my dapnacio: but
through thy mercy/to the helth of my soule/and
in the remyssyo of my synnes/through thy payn=
ful passyon. So be it.

℞ When thou hast recepued it.

Fiat perceptio cozpozis et sanguinis tui.

The very true recepuynge of thy glozyous
body of flesshe & bloude/my souereygne loz
de ofpoztet is/that J cast the not fozth agayne to
my dapnacyo & iudgemet/but that J may obtey=
ne therby remyssyo of my synnes: & that J may ly
ue in charytable lyfe/whyles J am here lyuyng/
so that J may here after come to the eternall ly=
fe/by thy vertue and grace.

℞ The prayer of saynt Bernardyne.

O bone Jesu/O dulcis Jesu.

O Bountefull Jesu. O swete Je
su. O iesu the sone of the pu=
re virgyn Mary: full of mercy and
trueth. O swete iesu/after thy gre
at mercy haue pyte vpo me. O be=
nygne iesu / J pray ꝰ by the same
pcyous bloude: whiche foz vs myse
rable synners/thou waste content
to shedde i the aulter of the crosse/that ꝰ vouch=
safe cleane to auoyde al my wyckednes/& not to

despyce me humbly this requyrynge/and vpon thy
moost holy name Iesus callynge. This name Iesꝰ/
is the name of helth. What is iesus/but a sauy=
our? O good iesu that hast me created:and with
thy pcious bloude redemed / suffre me not to be
dãpned/whõ of nought thou hast made. O good
iesu/let not my wyckednes destroye me/that thy
almyghty goodnes made & fourmed. O good ie=
su reknowledge that is thyn i me:and wype clea
ne away/that eloyneth me frõ the. O good iesu:
when tyme of mercye is/haue mercy vpõ me:noꝛ
destroye me not i tyme of thy terryble iudgemẽt.
O good iesu yf I a wretched syñer/foꝛ my moost
greuous offences/haue by thy very iustyce:deser=
ued eternall payne / yet I appell from thy very
ryghtuousnes/and stedfastly truste in thyne in=
effable mercye:so as a mylde father / and mercy=
full loꝛde oughte/take pytie vpon me. O good
Jesu/what pꝛofyte is in my bloude/syns that I
musle descende into eternall coꝛrupcyon? Cer=
teynly/they that ben deade shall not magnifye
the noꝛ lykewyse al they that go to hell. O moost
mercyfull iesu/ haue mercy vpon me. O moost
swete Jesu delyuer me. O moost meke Jesu / be
vnto me fauourable. O Jesu accept me a wret=
ched synner/ in to the nombꝛe of them that shal
be saued. O Jesu the health of them that be=
leue in the/haue mercy vpon me. O Jesu the
swete foꝛgyuenes of all my synnes. O Jesu the
sone of the pure virgyn Mary / endewe me
with thy grace/wysdom charyte/chastyte/and

humylyte:yea and in all myne aduersytes/stedfa
ste pacyēce:so that I may perfytely loue the/ and
in te to be glozyfyed/and haue my onely delyte in
the/worlde without ende. So be it.

Glozyous kynge/whiche amōgest thy sayn
tes arte laudable/ & neuerthelesse incōpera
ble. Thou arte in vs/lozde/& thy holy name hath
bē called vpō by vs. Therfoze do not forsake vs
lozd god/& in the day of iudgement vouchsafe to
bestowe vs among thy sayntes and electe.
O blyssed kynge.

A prayer vnto the ymage of the body of
Conditoz celi et terre.

Maker of heuē & earth kyng
of kynges/ & lozde of lozdes/
whiche of nothyng dyddest make
me to thy ymage & lykenesse/ and
dyddest redeme thyn owne bloude
whom I a synner am not wozthy
to name:neyther to call vpō/ney=
ther w my herte to thynke vpon/
hūbly I desyze the/ & mekely pzay
the/that gently thou beholde me/
thy wycked seruaūt/ & haue mercy on me/whiche
hadest mercy on the woman of Canane/ & of Ma
ry Magdalene/whiche dyddest fozgyue the Pu=
blycan / and the thefe hangynge on the crosse.
Unto the I confesse oh moost holy father / my
synnes/whiche yf I wolde/ I can not hyde from
the. Haue mercy on me Chzyste /foz I a wzetch
haue soze offended the/in pzyde/in couetousnes

in glotony/in lechery/in vaynglory/ī hatred/ in
enuy/in adultery/in thefte/in lyeng/in backeby
tynge/in sportyng/in dissolute and wantō laug=
hynge/in ydle wordes/in hearyng/in tastynge/in
touchynge/in thynkynge/in sleppynge/ī workyn
ge/and in always/in whiche I a frayle mā / and
mooste wretched synner myght synne. My defaul
te/my moost greuous defaulte. Therfore I moost
humbly pray and beseche thy gētylnesse/whiche
(for my health) descended from heuyn which dyd
holde vp Dauyd/that he shulde not fall in to syn
ne. Haue mercy on vs (O Christe) the whiche dy=
dest forgyue Peter/that dyd forsake thē. Thou
arte my creatour: & my helper/my maker/and my
redemer: my gouernour/and my father: my lorde:
my god: my kynge. Thou arte my hope/my trust:
my gouernour: my helpe: my cōfort: my strength:
my defence: my redempcyon: my lyfe: my health/
my resurreccyon. Thou art my stedfastnes/my re
fuge or succoure: my lyght: and my helpe. I moost
humbly and hertely desyre and praye the helpe
me: defende me: make me strong and confort me:
make me stedfast make me mery/gyue me lyght/
visyte me: reuyue me agayne whiche am deade.
For I am thy makynge/& thy worlke. Oh lorde:
despyce me not: I am thy seruaūte: thy bōde mā:
all though euyll: although vnworthy & a synner.
But what soeuer I am: whether I be good or
badde: I am euer thyne. Therfore to whome shall
I flye: except I flye vnto the? yf ȳ cast me of: who
shall or wyll receyue me. Yf ȳ despyce me: & turne

thy face frō me. Who shall loke vpō me? And re=
cognise ⁊ knowledge me (although vnworthy) cō=
mynge to the/altough I be vyle ⁊ vncleane. For
yf I be vyle ⁊ vncleane/thou canst make me cle=
ne. Yf I be sycke thou canst heale me. Yf I be dea=
de ⁊ buryed thou canst reuyue me. For thy mercy
is moche more thē myne iniquite. Thou canst for=
gyue me more thē I can offende. Therfore (oh lor=
de) do not ruder/nor haue respecte to the nōbre
of my synnes / but accordynge to the great=
nes of thy mercy forgyue me and haue mercy on
me moost wretched synner. Saye vnto my soule/
I am thy health whyche saydest/ I wyl not the
death of a synner/but rather that he lyue/and be
conuerted. Turne me oh lord: to the / and be not
angry with me/I pray the moost meke father/⁊
for thy great mercy/I moost humbly beseche the:
that thou bryng me to the blysse/that neuer shal
ceasse. So be it. ¶ A prayer for wysdō Sap.ix.

Deus patrum nostrorū/et dominus mie.

The god of our fathers god
of mercy whiche hast made
all wt thy worde/⁊ with thy wys=
dome haste constytuted man / to
haue dominyon vpon the creatu=
re whiche was made of the: to or=
der the world with equite and iu=
styce / ⁊ with a dyrecte herte for
to iudgementes/gyue me the as=
systent wysdome of thy seates/ and reproue me
not from thy chyldren. For thy seruaunt am I/⁊

ND - #0013 - 210423 - C0 - 229/152/9 [11] - CB - 9780265845073 - Gloss Lamination